THE DOG YEARS
OF
Ananias Zachenko

PAUL H LEPP

508 West 26th Street KEARNEY, NE 68848
402-819-3224
info@medialiteraryexcellence.com

TABLE OF CONTENTS

DEDICATION

TO MY BROTHER PETE...

UPFRONT YOU KNEW WE ARE HEART ATTACK PEOPLE, THIS IS THE STANDARD PROCEDURE OF HOW WE CHECK OUT OF HERE. BUT NO, YOU HAD TO BE DIFFERENT AND GET CANCER AND DIE. REMEMBER WHEN WE USED TO TALK, AND I'D TELL YOU SOMETHING AND A LOT OF TIMES YOU'D BEGIN YOUR REPLY WITH - "YOU HAVE NO IDEA..." AND GO INTO WHAT I HAD NO IDEA OF. TRY THIS ON FOR SIZE, HERE'S WHAT YOU HAVE NO IDEA OF - YOU HAVE ABSOLUTELY NO IDEA OF HOW MUCH I MISS YOU!! SURPRISINGLY I'M NOT ALONE BASED ON THE CROWD THAT SHOWED UP AT YOUR FUNERAL. ONE OF THESE DAYS I'LL CATCH UP WITH YOU AND YOU'LL FINALLY HAVE AN IDEA OF WHAT I'M TALKING ABOUT, AND WE'LL PICK UP WHERE WE LEFT OFF, AND AS USUAL, YOU'LL FIND OUT I DO KNOW WHAT I'M TALKING ABOUT AND ALWAYS HAVE...IT'S SUCH A DIFFERENT WORLD WITHOUT YOU... PAUL

AWARE

To kill the time in the waiting room it became a contest between the floor, walls and ceiling, he stared at one as much as the other as if he were planning an escape. He had no interest in the magazines on the coffee tables or the faces of those who browsed them. He didn't feel like a patient about to be treated, he felt like a prisoner about to be sentenced. And he knew why.

He was held captive by one thought, the notion of all the things he had worn out in his life: shoes, clothes, cars, tools, furniture, appliances, not to mention people and himself. The list went on and on, and he concluded it wasn't what one made in life, but what one wore out.

He reasoned as he waited, we're just a wristwatch on the arm of time and can only be wound so many times or wear down so many batteries. Springs unwind, batteries go dead, and we stop. A watch that never shows the same face twice when glanced at, to see how much time has been used or how much time is left. Always leaving one to wonder if it's the correct time. All the time wishing for more, other times wishing for less. Such were the thoughts of Ananias Zachenko, better known as "Chenko," as he entered the dog years of his life.

His turn came and Chenko got diagnosed. It took sixty-four years for all his bad habits to overrun the good ones, and the diagnosis shouldn't have surprised him, but it did. It was the death sentence. At best, he had one year and some change left. Chenko's first thought is to put a bullet through his head. From that moment on, the thought would come and go.

The terrorist cells were no longer underground, they had surfaced and were on the march towards just about every major organ but Chenko's heart. That's all he has left. The heart will have to find a way to keep pounding through the assaults. There will be onsets and remissions. But every organ overrun by the terrorist cells will die; eventually the organs will fail, and the heart will no longer have any purpose. At the rate the terrorists are moving, in a year or so Ananias Zachenko will no longer exist. This is what Chenko is told in so many words or what he hears.

The appointment he finally keeps reveals what past appointments could have prevented, had Chenko kept them. But if there was one thing, he was good at, it was breaking these appointments. If he felt okay, why go? Now he knows. When he got the news, and what he faced, his true nature surfaced in defiance not denial. There's a difference, 'defiance' is to resist or fight, 'denial' is to disregard or ignore.

For the most part he felt all right the day he was made aware of his condition and after the initial shock found his feet and felt as strong as ever. To blow his brains out was eventually replaced by a second thought.

The second thought was brought on by a trip to another waiting room to set up a treatment plan. As he drove, he conjured up in his mind the thirteenth century monks from Westminster Abbey, he had read about in another waiting room the previous week.

The monks began to observe their dogs and after a while put forth the idea that dogs age at a faster rate than humans. At first, they came up with a one to nine ratio where one human year was nine years in a dog's life. Continued observations made over time by the monks allowed them to adjust the ratio to one human year was seven years to a dog. After reading it what struck Chenko the most was it took thirteen centuries to figure this out.

He then pictured a fourteen-year-old boy who had a two-year-old dog. If you ask him the age of his dog the boy would answer in his years not dog years, he'd say "The dog is two," when comparatively he and the dog are the same age by the monk's ratio. From that appointment on whenever the 'white coats' brought up the year he had left he'd *dog year* it. The boy and his dog proved a 'year' to be an arbitrary measurement, it meant one thing for a human and another for a dog. Chenko muttered, "Why can't it be arbitrary for Ananias Zachenko?" And then answered his own question, "No reason."

He came to realize a dog year is fifty-two days not fifty-two weeks. There's the difference. The dog has a very compressed life when compared to humans. Being told he only has a year or so left would make the seven years in a dog year attractive until one learns how compressed they are. A day was a week in a dog year. Chenko couldn't get over the fact. What he needed to do was figure out a way to take the time in dog years off the daily and onto a weekly rate.

Chenko viewed his diagnosis as a sentence and as a death row inmate would make every appeal he could to buy more time. Yet, he didn't ignore certain facts. There's nothing permanent about us, no one gets out alive. Earth is a planet where all is temporary. Everyday some come, others go. It's a binary star of birth and death, everyone passes through a beginning and an ending. It's an 'ashes to ashes, dust to dust' deal.

However, for some strange reason Chenko's second thought, about the monks and their dogs, makes him think he may have more time than the white coats believe. He'll set a scale of time in his mind, in *his* years, with the lowest limit set at one year and the highest limit set at seven. This he feels is a rational approach. He'll be on the 'Weekly Dog Year Scale' as opposed to the 'Daily Dog Year Scale.' He takes the view that if the predicted end falls in the mid-range or above on the weekly scale it's a bonus. The search for answers for the situation he's in creates within him a target other than his head. This is his reaction to his diagnosis or sentence. Somehow, he'll figure out a way to decompress the dog years.

Chenko doesn't take it any further. To go any deeper, he believed, would be counterproductive, even though there is more depth to explore in setting the foundation to his logic. He doesn't care what he's been told or what the picture displays, he'll just come up with a method to manufacture more time by somehow converting dog years to human years to correct the situation. Hit mid-range or above, beat the odds, and use the time to leave the family in a good position.

His second thought provides the desire to come up with a balanced calculation to give him more time to carry out all that must be done before he dies. The second thought introduces both hope and desire which begin to suppress the first thought he had about the situation. The gun is getting farther from his head. Hope and desire become major constants in his equation for more time.

From here on out he doesn't plan on playing by the rules of time. He begins to question what is an hour? What is a day, week, month or year? He concludes they're not what we think. Each interval of time is interpreted as either going too fast or too slow; too fast if you're laughing and too slow if you're crying. Chenko becomes more aware of the emotions of time than its intervals. He begins his search for the meaning of time rather than the measurement of time. He looks for any method there is to lengthen the short leash he is on.

So, with his scale of possibilities and equation of hope and desire, he'll try to adjust time to his needs, where it moves neither too fast nor slow, Chenko will take the emotional time he has left and put his life in order.

How is it I know the thoughts of Ananias Zachenko? How is it I can tell you about the dog years? All I've seen? I'll tell you this... *Do not neglect to show hospitality to strangers, for thereby some have entertained angels unawares... Hebrews 13:02*

CHAPTER I: TIME

A nanias Zachenko began playing for time the day he was diagnosed. He set an agenda. Its purpose was to maximize the minimum time he's been told he has left to put his affairs in order. The program will be launched like a three-stage rocket. The *First Stage* will be the finances, which will involve calls, meetings and signatures. *Second Stage* will be informing the immediate family, close relations and good friends, which will involve visitations, conversations and goodbyes. The *Third Stage* will be the heroic act which will be the kindhearted departure.

The first will be easy, the second harder and the third hardest. Chenko is working on a calculation that will make time for all. Over time he'll plot his accomplishments against a scale he's set in his mind. He's far more interested from the day of his diagnosis on the firing order of his three-stage rocket. There won't be any bucket list of what he always wanted to do, only a list of what he needs to do. When the three stages carry out their mission, maybe then he'll find time to die.

The aerial view of Chenko reveals a complex terrain, but not a particularly rough or harsh landscape. It shows deep rivers of thought, a mountain range of concepts, and an open prairie of plans, all areas inhabited by good and bad ideas. There are prosperous regions that are well thought out and failing regions that have absolutely no thought behind them at all. The view from above shows these two regions are almost equivalent in size.

The ground view yields the highest resolution. On the ground, along with the terrain, one is also exposed to the inhabitants and their history. This exposure helps explain how the good and bad regions evolve in Chenko. From the ground exploration it's learned he was named Ananias after the one who was told to put his hands on Saint Paul's eyes so he could see. The name came from his mother and was accepted by his father, but it certainly wasn't his first choice, he wanted Isaac. The one God spared.

Chenko was born neither rich nor poor in the middle of 1948, June 21st in Akron, Ohio and grew up in Hidden Rocks, the younger of two brothers and a sister. In the family he is called "Nye." His brothers are also called "Chenko," but those from the neighborhood and those who know the Zachenkos refer to the oldest brother as "Sonny," the middle as "Jeep" and Nye as "Little Chenko." His sister is known as Helene after her mother and was given to her by her father. His father is known as "Ez," short for Ezra.

And those who know Nye or Little Chenko are aware he's friends with the seven deadly sins and only acquainted with the seven heavenly virtues. The sins are innate and come by free will and human nature, but he learned virtue and character from his parents. His mother wanted a good son and his father had unique ways to enforce her wishes. The genes each gave him developed Chenko into a cunning and compassionate person. He is good at trapping people, but he lets most go. The paradox these characteristics create is always in conflict within him. Always choosing the dark pieces on the board, he's willing to play chess with God. Always has.

At this point all Chenko can do is look at the board and move his pieces to pro-long, not avoid, the inevitable. Wondering what piece, like his organs, must be surrendered to postpone the checkmate. He'll take the maximum time the rules allow to make his next moves. This is all he knows now. This is what he concentrates on. The game has taken on a greater intensity.

Up to this point he's played a pretty steady game, but he's cornered. It's not that Chenko has underestimated his opponent. In the end he knows who will win; he just wishes he'd made more good moves than bad. He still has lots of friends around; the thought of getting taken out of the game this early bothers him. Almost as if he doesn't know how the game is played. His only strategy left is the dog years and the agenda he's set. He'll save face by the way he ends the game. That's what will be remembered. That and he took more time than he was given in the end.

*****

Chenko spent two months in actual dog years keeping his medical appointments. Eight meetings that sucked up eight days that fell randomly in the period of putting his finances in order. He found them more a hindrance than a help. Each led to another appointment, a new test, a prescription to be filled. There is a never-ending amount of paperwork. During this time, he keeps his wife, Ilene and two daughters, Eve and Hope, in the dark along with everyone on how these days are spent.

The random trips to the doctors are becoming harder and harder to cover up. The paperwork required by the medical field and the insurance industry is as voluminous as it is repetitive. Always a controversy of what is needed and what is covered. The side effects of the stress they provide make the cure worse than the disease.

After about eight appointments he has a fairly accurate picture medically of what is going on. It isn't a pretty or complete picture, but one to be studied. Soon he'll correct the picture by taking over his treatment. He becomes both doctor and patient in treating the condition. Chenko will decide how terminal he really is. Other than what he's been told, he feels no different than the day he was diagnosed.

These are his alternatives to the standard procedure. In the interest of time and to avoid the cover ups, paperwork, controversy and side effects, Chenko has started going to the health stores instead of the appointments. He buys products containing antioxidants in bulk, doubled up on his fruits, vegetables and has begun to exercise. He's changed this much.

Alcohol will always be in the cards, and it's too late to quit smoking. In fact, along with all his antioxidants, fruits and vegetables, exercise, he'll get a pound of weed to help stretch out the time. He'll have to look up Jimmy Chesterfield. What region of the mind, good or bad, this idea comes from doesn't matter. Chenko rationalizes. What was this approach going to do? Kill him? He decides he isn't going to be part of the lost patrol in the war of procedure and coverage.

After his eighth doctor's appointment, takes this new approach to his remaining time. It comes down to this: the white coats in Akron can't do any more for him; he'll have to go up the road and talk to the ones in Cleveland. First the little pyramids of winding hallways and hidden rooms in Akron, then the big pyramids of Cleveland. All the therapy he receives during the eight days, or two dog months come from the traffic jams and waiting rooms he finds himself in. Oddly enough, through all his comings and goings, Chenko becomes a more patient person, using the time to reflect on the past and plan the future.

The morning of the last appointment Chenko kept, he grabs a gym bag he always called his 'satchel' and makes his way to where he has parked for the last thirty years feeling no different than he did the first time he went to his side of the garage. The feeling of running late.

When they'd built the house Chenko thought he had more than enough garage for his wife and him. The years have proved him wrong. Shelves overflow with Christmas decorations, plastic garbage cans filled with badminton racquets, bats and basketballs along with tents, sleds, bikes, chainsaw, lawn mower, barbeque and garbage can. All the big, miscellaneous stuff is found on his side of the garage. On his wife's side, flowerpots are stacked in orderly fashion, on a potting table, hanging on a wall next to it, are all the gardening tools. By the steps leading into the house are the recycle bins.

Both are territorial when it comes to their side of the garage. Ilene's side is easily seen from the street, she has no fear of leaving the garage door up on her side. What she does fear is an invasion from Nye's side where the garage door is to always be down.

Chenko drops his keys on his way to the truck. As he bends over to pick them up, he subconsciously places the satchel in an open space on one of the shelves. On top of this he pushes it to the back of the shelf when he temporarily loses his balance standing up.

After regaining his balance Chenko climbs into his mid-size red Ford truck, which is in fair shape given the time Chenko has owned it, relieved he didn't have to kiss the concrete floor. His actions are simultaneous and sub-conscious once inside as he reaches for a cigar and fires up both the truck and the cigar at the same time unaware of what he did with the satchel.

He backs up lost in the thought of how many trucks he's had. Old Red is his fifth, he recalls, as some begin to flash across his mind, but isn't sure. What he is sure of is he's been good at running everyone into the ground after about five or six years, Ford or Chevy. This could be the sixth, but he isn't in the mood to find the one he might be missing. At the end of the driveway he comes to a stop, puts Old Red in drive, gives it some gas, thinking he's had this truck the longest and it seems to run the best of all. It makes him smile, like he finally got it right.

Next Chenko concerns himself with the truck's gauges. Every truck he owned had gauges, no idiot lights. The needle on the battery is leaning a little negative, but okay. The needle on the Oil pressure bounces around for a moment but finally finds the middle of the gauge and there is a quarter of tank of gas. Chenko must make the first decision of the day - gas up before breakfast or after? He chooses after.

In fact, as he thinks about it, he may not need to get gas. His thoughts turn to the number of deuce-and-a-halfs he'd driven on "E" over Highway 19 in the Central Highlands, through the An Khe Pass or up in Kontum when he was in the Army. He studies the gas gauge for a moment and believes he has enough fuel for the ground he has to cover. It would be tight, always is. But then Chenko has been trained to run on empty. "Gas up tomorrow," He decides. Even though he's aware it isn't the most prudent decision. Once it's made Chenko exhales a cloud of smoke, turns on the radio and heads to Betty's for breakfast.

Chenko has been blessed in many ways, one being he can burn up what he takes in and maintain proper vital signs and weight with minimum effort. In a way this blessing is a major contributor to the condition he's now in. It's led to excesses most don't get to enjoy without paying a penalty physically or mentally up front. Up to now Chenko was an exception to the rule. He looks to be in better shape than he actually is. He's strong but could be stronger if he wasn't always in touch with his vices.

On the way he checks some other gauges that concern him. Like the truck he thinks is running okay. This morning the dashboard in his head made him aware his weight was gradually starting to go down instead of up considering his intake. He has a long deep scratch from a rose bush on the outside of his upper left leg that should have healed by now. Something is going on. Chenko winces, not in pain, but from the knowledge. So far there's been no pain and he wonder how long it will be before that kicks in and what he'll do then. The thought leaves him as fast as it arrived when he pulls into Betty's.

There isn't a server who doesn't know Chenko at Betty's. Every one of them has been through his routine and knows it by heart. He prefers the back corner booth, but will take a table. Once he's seated there's no telling what he may say after they ask "The usual?" If he has time Chenko will answer "I don't know... What would you get?" The veterans roll their eyes and answer "The usual." The rookie will recite the menu at least twice before they catch on, he always orders two poached eggs, bacon, rye toast, a cup of fruit and coffee. He'll also try to tell them the exact order in which the food should arrive at his table. All have felt the urge to just slap him after waiting on him, same with the tellers at the bank. Yet the times he doesn't show up as expected they're the first who want to know where he's been.

The morning of the last appointment he would ever go to and, the last paperwork he would ever turn in up in Cleveland, Chenko was running behind. He barked "The usual!" At the first waitress within earshot. Her name is Audrey and barking doesn't work with her. Chenko backs right off once he sees the target he's hit. He puts his arms up in mock surrender and adds in a soothing voice "When you have time." She then smiles the smile that lets him know he's come to his senses and points to the back corner booth as she checks her other eight to ten customers for coffee refills.

Chenko makes his way to the booth, nodding to the customers he passes and Audrey soon fills his cup with coffee asking "What's new, Chenko?"

"If you only knew..." he answers. Thinking he will fill her in, which she is strangely in the mood for, Chenko instead lifts the cup to his lips, looks away and says nothing more. She smiles, but he doesn't see it. She then clears a table close to the booth before putting his order in and notices Chenko isn't watching her like he always does; she's in the mood for that too.

There's no protest to what she's doing like she expects and she mentions it to Melody, the other waitress, "What's with Chenko?" Melody jokes, "I don't know. Maybe he's gone blind. Hard not to notice how tight your jeans are!" Audrey playfully shoves her aside and heads to the kitchen informing them, "Chenko is in his booth."

This is all the kitchen needs to know. Nothing is in writing and as always, they'll have to remember. Sometimes they take care of the usual right away. Other times it goes to the bottom of the list and occasionally, they forget.

The way the morning is playing out the usual wouldn't show up right away. Chenko is okay with this. He wants to use the time to figure out a way around a thorny issue. He has some property he now wants to sell, he has a buyer and could get a good price, but the transaction requires Ilene's signature. He wants to finagle a way to complete the sale without her knowing what is going on. Wants to put that off for as long as possible, yet at the same time he has to move fast on this deal. The situation needs a solution.

He becomes agitated with the issue and decides to take it outside. He'll fight with it out in the parking lot and have another smoke, something he usually doesn't do while waiting for 'the usual,' but this isn't a normal morning. Chenko takes a binary approach to the problem. "There are two solutions out there, first: get the signature, second: forge it. One is better than the other; one is easier than the other. One is legal, the other illegal." Chenko begins to weigh the pros and cons of each as he finds his way to an unoccupied bench Betty has placed outside for her smoking clientele. He unwraps a cigar throws the wrapper in large pail of sand filled with the dead matches, torn wrappers and crushed butts of those who have preceded him. It's not a scenic area, but an area he's comfortable in.

As he sits there smoking, a warm breeze wafts by and his thoughts are blown off course. The breeze with its scent and motion recalls a time in his life fifty years ago, fifty-two to be exact. The sun wrestles with the clouds, bright one moment and dark the next, not unlike the day a certain event happened; it too was warm with a nice breeze occasionally between the light and dark.

He settles comfortably into the bench and sees himself the time he was twelve, the last year before becoming teenager. He's standing in the wooded rolling hills and grassy meadows of the Cuyahoga Valley. At a place called Camp Manitoc, a Boy Scout. The time and place he demonstrates a power given him.

It was a small power, but a power just the same. And beyond his family few knew about it until that day. From about the age of six on, at picnics, hiking, or camping all Chenko heard was "Do you know you're standing in poison ivy?" Or "Get out of the poison ivy!" One was given in shock by those who thought he didn't know. The other was given as a threat by those who knew he did know. At an early age he put two and two together and at such events it is the first thing he looks for.

At an early age it became apparent he could expose himself to what others feared and never pay the price. He never got poison ivy. Not until about twenty-two when he rubbed the leaves into his left forearm to impress and scare his brother Jeep at a family reunion. Seems Jeep could get it by just looking at it. About three days later Chenko got it and now gets like everyone else. It makes his bother happy.

Chenko inwardly chuckles at the visions and mutters, as he exhales a cloud of smoke. "Well at least I landed on my feet when it was over..." in response to the memory, calling to mind the doubt he had at the time. He returns to the time, place and group he went public with the power he once had.

The troop Chenko is in has four patrols of at least twelve to thirteen guys. It's the late Fifties, early Sixties and Scouting is popular and viewed as a proper, almost required activity for the development of young men. During this time several troops are at platoon strength. The vast majority of them church sponsored, meeting one day a week, usually in the church basements. If your parents belonged to a church back then there was a fifty-fifty chance the young men from ages eleven to sixteen were Scouts. The chance of the adult male leadership being veterans would be the same. His parents met these unwritten requirements and his older brothers had been scouts. It seemed to work and Chenko would be no different than his brothers.

It's Chenko's second camp. Summer camp lasts a week. The time is spent earning badges and making rank. The day comes along when maps and compasses are used to find a far-off location. That day they each dress in jeans and tee-shirts, put on backpacks and full canteens. Compasses and maps in hand they gather under the flag of their patrol. They set out at equal distance, but from different directions to find a mythical Indian Village.

For the most part each patrol was on their own, the adults at two check points on each route and at the village. The Otters and Beavers become hopelessly lost and some of the adults are pulled to find them, eliminating a checkpoint on each route. The less supervised Buffalos and Bears are left to their own devices to see who will take the village first.

It was after the checkpoint that the Buffalo patrol saw the Bear patrol off in the distance crossing a clearing. The Bears didn't see the Buffalo's. The Scout's first instinct was to call out to them, but then a stronger instinct took hold to keep their position unknown. The Bears were at a right angle to the Buffalos and about a half-mile away. Each patrol was about a mile away from the village. The Bears were making good time through the clearing. The Buffalos needed a plan to move faster or find a way to hold up the other patrol. All the Buffalos knew the terrain they faced was against fast and all began to concentrate on the second option, the hold up.

The Bears were a problem. Every Buffalo knew the Bears had at least two guys who could walk through any four guys they put up against them. They couldn't stop them physically. A discussion of sending a couple of guys out to set a small "controlled" fire in their path while the rest of the patrol moved on to the village came under consideration. They concluded that the Bears would have to stop and put it out. Whoever went out would then catch up with tail end of the patrol and be viewed as stragglers as opposed to arsonists. And that could be done, what the Buffalo's lacked in strength they could make up in speed.

The decision to go with the fire is almost made when Chenko sees the poison ivy and the solution. While the others prepare for "operation Bear fire" gathering up their matches and making kindling he makes his way to the poison ivy and grabs two handfuls. By the time he returns all are starting to second guess the tactic, each asking themselves "What if the fire gets out of control? Who'll light it?" But no one is talking and, no one is volunteering. Chenko stands in their silence and waits for their gasps. They don't disappoint him when they notice what he has in his hands and instinctively begin to back away. Recognizing the power he has, Chenko jabs at them to demonstrate what he has, what they have.

"This is how we'll do it!" Chenko announces. He explains how he'll get in front the Bears, as planned. He'll pick a spot and instead of going through with the fire use the ivy. Anyone coming in contact with him will get the ivy. No one is blind to the weapon they now have. The Buffalos come up with a warhead and delivery system. They have their deterrent. No one wants to get the ivy. No one also is blind to the fact with the fire all could get in trouble, with the ivy only Chenko. His plan is authorized immediately.

And that's what happens; Chenko runs in front of the Bears and intercepts them at a small creek where he holds them off. He holds them up long enough for the Buffalos to take the village first. Long enough that Mr. Claybaugh and Mr. Goldsborough are sent to find the missing Bears and Chenko when no one in the Buffalos will accurately explain where Chenko is and if they saw the missing patrol.

Mr. Claybaugh and Mr. Goldsborough are veterans of the second big one and are both amused and amazed at what they come across by the creek and find the Bears and Chenko. It reminds them of similar, but far more deadly, situations they'd been in. The delaying action of the lethally camouflaged Chenko with grenade in hand is not lost on them. Besides neither has a kid in the Bears.

Chenko has trapped the Bears at a narrow crossing. He can't be out flanked. Two rock walls on the right and left give him the advantage. The Bears will have to cross the stream and go at him head on. A target covered in poison ivy, wound around chest and arms, woven through his belt loops, a camouflaged enemy soldier now out in the open on the other side of the creek fifteen to twenty feet from them. There he stands giving them enough distance to stop and recognize what they are up against.

He stands defiant holding a tube that once held his tooth brush now half-filled with water, telling them it's the plant's venom. There he is in front of the Bears holding a five-foot opening, capable of making contact with, most of them, if not all, if he has to, forcing the Bears to reconsider any quick direct assault. He's teasing the Bears who can't wait to get their hands on him, as soon as he is clean. But this isn't going to happen. His safety is guaranteed by two adults who show up and seem to be more on Chenko's side than the trapped patrol. He surrenders to Mr. Claybaugh and Mr. Goldsborough releasing the Bears.

Chenko receives a hero's welcome from the Buffalos, Otters and Beavers when the lost patrol makes it to the village. As that afternoon drifts into early evening and with three out four guys in his corner, the Bears drop their vendetta, and all in the troop want to know about the power Chenko has over the ivy. Chenko spins stories about it, not having any idea how to explain something he himself doesn't understand, at times over playing his hand.

Chenko pulls on his cigar and repositions himself on the bench, then exhales, lost in the past. There would be a Court of Awards soon after they return from camp. Three weeks to be exact. Two meetings reviewing the cards turned in for badges and rank. Chenko has five merit badges coming and a jump in rank. He looks forward to Court. Everything on his end is fine; he has medicine man status among his peers now that camp is over. At the time he never doubted he'd get what was rightfully his.

However, among some of the adults his exploits at camp take on warlock status. Two in particular, Mr. Kang and Mr. Rich made what happened at the creek an issue and launch a full-blown investigation. The outcome of the investigation leads to a special meeting of the adult leadership, the topic Chenko. Mr. Kang and Mr. Rich exploiting the chemical warfare the Bears faced that day. Unlike Mr. Claybaugh and Mr. Goldsborough their sons were in the patrol. Their sons and the other Bears were exposed to a serious threat and Mr. Kang and Mr. Rich or any other good parents should not turn a blind eye to what happened. It was fortunate Mr. Claybaugh and Mr. Goldsborough came along when they did. Who knows what could've happened? Ezra Zachenko is informed and told to attend the meeting.

Chenko is unaware, still looking forward to the Court of Awards. After his father is informed, he is then made aware there might not be any awards and he might no longer be a member of the troop. Chenko's world goes from one of no doubt to one filled with doubt. The situation is explained to him by Ez after work one night when Chenko is ordered into his Ez's 1960 Ford Fairlane 500, that has a powder blue body and navy-blue roof with white walls, and made to return to the scene of the crime to see what it may offer in defense of the situation both find themselves in.

On the way there Ezra Zachenko listens to his son and says little as Chenko explains what happened. Chenko's anger begins to overtake him as he details the plans for a "controlled" fire and the alternative he proposed. Ez starting to shake his head but let his son vent, since no one is around to hear the now threatening and defiant Chenko, wondering how to handle the attitude of his son.

When they arrive at the scene Chenko once again, only with more anger, reiterates what he said in the car. "See - we didn't burn down the woods! And no one got the ivy! Those guys are a bunch of crybabies! They lost and now are trying to make it look like they won, and first chance I get Bud Kang and Eddy Rich are going to pay! This is a little deal they're trying to make a big deal!" Chenko ends.

Ez makes a mental note about the plans for the fire and the fact no one got poison ivy, and agrees with all his son has said except the part about getting even with Bud and Eddy and that situation they now find themselves isn't a "little deal." He lets his son know if he does anything to the two, he'll answer to him. Ez says this through clenched teeth in a low seething voice to inform Chenko this is no idle threat and is something to avoid at all cost. He ended with the same tone: "If this was a little deal, we wouldn't be standing here." Ez's inflection is not lost on his son.

As they leave the scene Ez orders Chenko to take one of his shoes and socks off, didn't matter which. Chenko is puzzled and asks "Why?" There's no answer, just the look. Chenko soon begins to do what he is told and chooses his right shoe and sock. Ez picks up a very small pebble, a jagged piece of white quartz and puts it Chenko's shoe. "Let me show you how something small can turn into something big," and orders Chenko to put the shoe with the stone minus the sock back on his foot for the half mile trek back to the car.

Nothing more is said as they walk to the car, the stone sliding back and forth from the ball to the heel of the foot, lacerating some of the soft flesh. It's like having a razor blade in his shoe. When they get to the car Chenko is allowed to remove the stone and put on the sock. Chenko and Ez leave the scene. By the time they get home Chenko has a bloody sock as a souvenir of their time together. A reminder of a power he abused.

Chenko only hears second hand accounts of how the meeting went. From these accounts Mr. Kang and Mr. Rich had some allies, but not a majority. Nothing they brought up helps Chenko's reputation, as one to be watched. To sway the attendees' and make their view the majority position they become emotional in making their case that the Zachenkos should have let everyone know about their son's immunity to poison ivy and his behavior when he's around it. They stated in the end some have died from poison ivy and that if Chenko wasn't dismissed from the troop there was good chance they would withdraw their sons advising others to do the same.

Chenko is told Ez waited his turn and tried to show as little emotion as possible to what was being said, but was not able to suppress all his emotions. Early in the meeting, after it was said his son should be watched Ez sat with both forearms on the table leaning over them with the balls of his feet positioned under his chair like a sprinter. It reminded him too much of some of the bad memories of his youth in the old country. The posture he assumed could be taken more than one way. He wanted it to be perceived as one of complete attention, but also as one that left little doubt how fast he could strike if had to.

When Ez spoke, he became less threatening by leaning back and making sure he made eye contact with all at some point. He spoke in terms of what did happen as opposed to what could have happened. He never brought up the fire, although talk about the plan was well known, he knew no one there wanted to conceive what could have happened if that plan went awry, especially the parents of the Buffalos. Letting his audience sub-consciously draw the conclusion between the ivy and the fire, the ivy was the better choice.

His appeal followed the lines of the All-American "no harm, no foul" defense letting his audience entertain the fact that not one boy came back from camp with poison ivy.

Secondly, based on the cards that had been turned in, the camp had been more productive than the previous year. In the end, Ez footnoting conditions and behaviors mentioned earlier, using as an example bed wetting, knowing as did everyone else, Eddy Rich was a victim of the condition. He challenged the opposition to reconsider their position about how open everything should be about the members of the troop.

What Chenko hears, he hears from others and the doubt is taken away. What Ez said was enough to carry the day. The vote was close, but in the end Chenko remained with the troop, even receives his awards. Bud and Eddy stay also, but their parents never miss an opportunity to keep the incident alive to an ever-shrinking audience. His father never provides any details of the meeting.

Chenko butts his smoke. Smiles and heads back to his booth, glad to have taken the time to revisit these recollections. But for the most part he is confused as to why they show up and what they mean. What seems vaguely clear from long ago, the three phases of doubt: when he had no doubt, was filled with doubt and then the doubt was taken away, as the possible reason behind it all. Something he could keep in the back of his mind and use to find the formula he's after. The satisfaction he feels from reliving the past leaves him with a new view about his current doubts. At that moment, it's enough for him to sit down and enjoy 'the usual' even though he is supposed to be running out of time.

******

The surface of Betty's parking lot is far from smooth. Between the door and Chenko's truck there's a deep puddle still filled with the previous night's rain. Taking a straight path to the truck, Chenko pays no attention to the surface and steps in it. The water covers his right foot up to the ankle. It's enough to break the spell of the time, place and group that held him captive through breakfast.

He shakes his head, but doesn't swear verbally, but in his mind. Then shakes his right foot and gets in the truck. For a moment he thinks of going home and changing socks. He mutters "It'll be dry by the time I make Cleveland," fires up the truck and the cigar. While leaving the parking lot he notices the small gym bag he keeps all his paperwork in is missing. He likes to call it his "satchel" it has the look that at one time it might have been used in a bank heist. It doesn't take long to figure out where it is. The bag from junior high is at home on the kitchen counter.

He brings the truck to a stop in the middle of the lot while he decides, along with the socks, if the satchel is enough to make him go home. The socks and satchel aren't enough; "Cleveland is going to have to deal with my wet foot and no paperwork today," he sighs and heads in that direction. He reminds himself "Have to nurse the gas," and gently steps on the accelerator with his wet foot.

Chenko is never on time for anything. Aware of this all his life, all the clocks he sets are set ahead by thirty-three minutes. A half hour cushion for every appointment, extra three minutes to be three hundred yards from any explosion. Even with the cushion he's always running late. He looks at the clock on the dashboard and calculates in an hour he has to be in Cleveland. He'll have to do eighty to make it on time, and he seriously doubts he can do that. There's no way he's going home now and no way to be on time. Figures he'll be fifteen to twenty minutes late. But it doesn't matter because it always takes a half-hour to an hour from the appointment time to get in with whoever he needs to see. In a way he figures he has an hour-an-half to two hours and actually will be early.

In Youngstown Jimmy Chesterfield has already left for Cleveland and by chance will meet with Chenko up the road. Chenko knows him from grade school. Jimmy was in the Sunshine class. There were eight grade schools in Hidden Rocks and one Sunshine class. At the time all the kids who weren't considered normal were kept in the basement of General Grade School. The school Chenko and Jimmy attended. Along with the normal kids Chenko knew all the "village idiots."

They were easy targets and if one good thing can be said about Chenko, it is that he never took advantage of any of them. His mother once told him they may be angels and God watches how one treats his angels. His father told him they got dealt bad cards for the hand they have to play; for them nothing on the table comes easy. Jimmy wasn't like most in these respects, he just couldn't read back then, he was dyslexic. Jimmy didn't get an education in school; he got it on the streets.

The problem with Jimmy back then he took advantage of his own kind. Chenko met him the first time after he watched Jimmy beat up poor LeEtta Krick for her lunch money. The fight that followed was harder than Chenko anticipated, but he made his point in the end. Jimmy never forgot it, even though the resume of the fights Jimmy's won over time is far more impressive than Chenko's. Yet, with all his faults, which are numerous, he and Chenko become good friends even though they come from different sides of the street. Together they've worked some deals.

One that comes to mind, the forged draft cards they sold to the juniors and sophomores when Chenko was a senior. Jimmy should have been a senior, but was a sophomore. The office of Hidden Rocks High School in early 1965 got their first Xerox copier. The secretaries preferred to continue to mimeograph and the new technology wound up in the art department. The art department had room for it until the secretaries either learned to use it or they got new secretaries. For a while the copier caused some controversy within the administration.

Art was the only class Chenko and Jimmy ever took together. As a side project to what they were supposed to be doing the two learned how to work the copier, embracing the new technology. It wasn't that Chenko chose his draft card to copy when they were playing around with the copier and the different types of paper that would pass through it, it just happened to be the first thing pulled from his wallet. They could put a similar heavyweight paper through it as a draft card. Once they both saw what they had, it was a short time before they got their hands on some white-out and a paper cutter. They would've preferred driver's licenses, but the green paper they had, had problems moving through the copier and wasn't a good match. The draft card was black and white and had no problems moving through the copier.

Sales were brisk over a one-week period. They both netted one hundred twenty dollars by the end of the week at ten dollars a card. It came to an end for Chenko one morning when Mr. Durkin, the assistant principal, called both to the office and asked what they knew about the fake daft cards. "You ever read the back of your draft card?" he asked. Neither had so he read them the penalty for forging one and it was stiff. Both sat in front of him trying to look like they had no idea why he was talking to them.

He then let them go. Nothing more was said. The juniors who got picked up in Kent over the weekend told the police they got them from some guys at school, but told their unit principal, after the school was dragged in, they got them from some guys who went to *another* school, some guy named Fairfield. They did this not out of fear of Chenko, but Chesterfield who at the time was building quite a resume of what happened to people who crossed him.

Chenko could see Mr. Durkin was building a case and told Jimmy "It's just a matter of time." There was no doubt in his mind and he got out of the operation, but Jimmy kept it up until he got caught. He got burned pretty bad, but never once mentioned Chenko through all the interrogations. Chenko has never forgotten this. The only thing Jimmy will say to others when it's brought up is "I should've listened to Chenko."

Chenko heads up Route Seventy-seven going a constant ten miles over the speed limit until he hits the Akron interchange, slowing down to head west to make the northern connection to Cleveland. As he builds up speed on the west leg, he is thinking about all the signed paperwork in the satchel that must be turned in but won't and the problems it will cause. He counts at least seven of his signatures held in the satchel and thinks to himself "I should get a rubber stamp!" At that moment it comes to him and he shouts out loud in his excitement as if he has someone who's listening... "Get a check Ilene has signed and get a rubber stamp made. Let someone else do the forgery! I'll only have to use it once!" The problem created by the satchel may be the solution to the land deal.

Five miles up the road a semi has lost a load of cantaloupes. The west end of the expressway becomes a parking lot. Chenko is lost in his excitement which soon changes to panic when he notices the traffic in front of him is stopped. He's back to top speed when he makes this discovery and has very short runway to control Old Red. Chenko has to stand on the brakes and squeals to a stop- inches from the rear end of a silver BMW.

From the moment the squealing starts the drivers all around him wonder about the outcome. After Old Red stops rocking back and forth, he takes a few moments before looking at those who witness his escape. Eventually he motions to the car in front of him by putting both hands in the air as a sign of surrender and apology. The woman breaks eye contact from her rear-view mirror after the gesture, shakes her head and has nothing more to do with him. The guy to his right doesn't want to be involved and looks straight ahead never making eye contact.

When Chenko looks to his left, at a slightly rusting beat-up white Hummer covered in 'Tap Out,' 'Everlast,' 'No Fear,' 'Grateful Dead,' 'Venom,' 'Semper Fi' and other decals and stickers of similar nature too numerous to mention, along with a bumper sticker, not on the bumper, but on the right-side rear window that reads *"If Jesus had a gun, he would have never been crucified."* Chenko doesn't know what to make of the collage or the guy behind the wheel.

The guy behind the wheel has the advantage. He makes Chenko out during his surrender to the BMW. But all Chenko sees is a guy, in a black shirt covered with skulls, bald on top with the hair on the sides swept back in a long grey pony tail looking right at him. Under an equally grey Fu Manchu mustache Chenko catches a menacing grin backed up by the finger. Chenko blinks two or three times trying to put it together, then begins to stare, he knows this guy and it comes as a relief when he finally makes Jimmy Chesterfield and he returns the grin and finger.

Nothing is moving. Chenko shuts the engine off and rolls down the window. The time he's losing is secondary to who he's actually run into. Jimmy's has been shut down for a while, but he starts his Hummer and pulls up two or three feet to align his right passenger window with Chenko. Hits the button to lower the window, but nothing happens, wrestles his way to the passenger seat and bangs on it until finally the window slides down like the blade of a guillotine.

Chenko shouts "Fairfield! … (The inside nickname few know was given to Jimmy by Chenko during the draft card days. Jimmy has always been okay with it, in fact on occasion uses it as an alias like he did back then) The door ate your window!" and starts to laugh not at the window, but at fate. Jimmy starts, "Never done that before," excusing his window and then goes into a long drawn out "Hay – Zeee!" (Jimmy's nickname for Chenko, a play on the word 'hazy' using Chenko's initials A. Z.), laughing at the same fate. It's been a while since they crossed paths.

"Man, you look terrible!" Jimmy continues. And for a brief moment Chenko fears he's been found out, that he must be sick, that if Jimmy is picking up on it, everyone has to know and starts to question his condition. He feels weak and unsure of himself, but gathers his composure. "No, man - You're catching yourself in the side mirror." Jimmy and Chenko trade insults, but nothing more is said about how each look, they both know they look the same. The doubt the moment brings is eventually lost in the exchange.

Jimmy has a cage fighter and asks Chenko what he knows about the cage. Chenko nods. "Catch it now and again." Jimmy then asks "Billy 'Battlefield' Brown, ever catch him?" Chenko shakes his head side to side. "Well, you will! I own him! I'll be in Cleveland next month, going there now to close the deal!"

Chenko lets Jimmy go through every fight the guy has had and how Jimmy found him in a parking lot one night beating the hell out of three guys. How Jimmy is developing him and the big payday down the road. Through it all Chenko smiles and says little, letting Jimmy enjoy the moment. He kids him about putting in the fix and Jimmy smiles. "Not now. Maybe later."

"I'll get you tickets – you'll see!" Jimmy continues. The truck door swings open and Chenko prepares to tell Jimmy, along with the tickets, what he'd really appreciate. "Oh! I got something better than that," Jimmy informs Chenko. "Not looking to blow my head off, just want to take the edge off," Chenko informs Jimmy. Jimmy nods. "Okay." A deal is made, the price is set, phone numbers are exchanged and a meeting set up.

After this they spend the remaining time going down memory lane and catching up with each other before traffic slowly begins to move. When Jimmy asks what Chenko has going on, Chenko answers, "Been making calls, setting up meetings, getting signatures." Jimmy asks "For what?" "You'll find out soon enough," Chenko answers with a somber smile that confuses Jimmy, but says nothing more even though Jimmy keeps pushing for an answer. When the traffic starts to move the two extend their arms from their window and clasp hands, the grip firm like their friendship until speed and direction pull them apart as Chenko's lane starts to move first.

Chenko's efforts the morning of the last appointment has mixed results; had he been on time and had his paperwork he wouldn't have had to reschedule most of what was to be done. However, the news he gets from what is done, is that nothing has gotten better or worse. The stage is the same. Chenko looks at it as a win. He thinks along with this he also has the 'rubber stamp' solution to the land deal, and a shipment coming in from Jimmy Chesterfield to help him down the road. He notices his foot is dry and thinks to himself, "It's been a good morning."

******

Chenko sits in W. Quentin Kaloon's office waiting for him to return from an appointment. It's one of the rare times he's early. He knows he'll have a long wait; Billy Kaloon is worse than Chenko when it comes to being on time. Ordinarily Chenko would be long gone if it were someone he didn't know or like. But Billy Kaloon has been Chenko's lawyer for over thirty years, a friend even longer.

Chenko sits in Billy's chair playing with the knick-knacks on his desk. Billy's desk is massive and for the most part clear of paperwork, it has the executive look. Chenko laughs at what is in front of him and mutters "Clear desk, empty mind." On the paneled oak walls are framed degrees, certificates of achievement, certificates of appreciation and memberships. Billy has the office every lawyer wants. He's all country-club and there's no reason he and Chenko should be friends, but they are.

The ice between them was broken at a party when Chenko mentioned that he knew a lot of guys who went to Ohio University; Billy the first he ever knew that graduated from the place. Billy has always viewed Chenko as someone who'll roll the dice, who lives at the foot of the cross and pays his bills. He's good for business.

Billy handled Chenko's case with the township when he tore out the temporary turn-around on his property. Chenko was building his house and used it as backfill for his driveway. Chenko argued it was township property on private property, if he did anything it was demonstrate how "temporary" the turn-around was. Billy won the case in spite of Chenko. For some reason the success brought him a lot of business.

Then there was the time Chenko got hit by a semi on Route Seventy-Seven and should have been killed, but was fine, he got Chenko a new Blazer and made a ton of money from the contingency agreement the two had. Chenko told him he was fine and only wanted the Blazer to be replaced and what he got above it he could keep. It was easy money for the work, Billy got as much as Chenko.

Ethel, Billy's office assistant, knows Chenko from Ilene. Ethel and Ilene belong to the same charitable and social organizations. She's the one allowing Chenko in Billy's office. She's done a few Christmas parties with the Zachenko's. Any conversation with Chenko always ends with "I really feel sorry for Ilene." Chenko doesn't rest in any update on Ilene until he hears it.

After it is finally said she offers Chenko some coffee. Chenko asks "Who made it you or Billy?" She just repeats the offer "You want coffee?" Chenko nods. She brings it to him and sweeps his feet off Billy's desk shaking her head on the way out saying nothing more.

She likes Chenko; more than once she's seen him give money to any poor soul who asked on the street, always giving a pat on the shoulder or back instead of a lecture or sermon. His "Take care," sincere. She knows Chenko's true gift is he can talk to anyone from the street to the country club, and she really doesn't feel sorry for Ilene.

The coffee is too hot to drink. Chenko places it on the desk and waits for it to cool, watching the steam rise from the brim and begins to try to solve a mystery. The satchel wasn't on the counter when he returned from the last appointment. It will take some time before he realizes it's camouflaged on the shelf with the Christmas decorations, the last place he put it while wrestling his way to Old Red. At the moment it's still a mystery to him; he's searched the house over and over again and walks right by it every time he gets in Old Red.

A lawyer's office would be the perfect place to solve the mystery and he begins concentrating. Like Betty's bench, his concentration on where it might be is overcome by the concentration of how it came to be, showing up on a birthday. All the places it's been with him. Junior high, high school, college, Army, marriage, kids; the satchel was always there. What it now held was secondary to the satchel itself. He wanted it back the same way he wanted the time back when he carried it through all these places.

If anything, positive is to come from the dilemma, Chenko decides he won't leave the planet until he knows where it is, it takes too much time. The thought of all this time being lost Chenko won't accept. This is all the further he can take it; he's not going anywhere until the satchel is found. It's not that he'll take more time to find it; it's that he'll make more time to find it.

Billy Kaloon returns to find Chenko in his chair. He sighs and tells Chenko, "I forgot all about you," as Chenko gets out of the chair, he tells Billy "I'm hurt! But that's okay if this meeting is the only thing, you forgot and nothing else. I'll forget you as soon it's over and everything is in order, so we're even."

Again, Billy sighs as he takes some papers from his brief case. "These are the papers you brought me," and starts to explain each. Chenko interrupts "Nothing goes to probate, right?" Billy nods. The papers are signed, all but the land deal. Billy stops in the middle of his explanations of what's been done, and asks "What's up Chenko?" Chenko smiles, then laughs "The jig."

CHAPTER II: SPACE

In the space of three weeks all of Chenko's finances are in order with the exception of the land deal. Five months in dog years. He's fortunate he's retired. Ilene works and the kids are out of the house. The deals generate mail, phone calls and messages, all of which Chenko has been able to intercept. He knows it's just a question of time before one gets through and spawns all the questions he doesn't want to answer.

Chenko tries to keep current on his bills, but it's a flawed system with several parties involved who do nothing but add confusion to every transaction. He mails checks and gives his credit card number, but as soon as one fire is out another starts. The insurance industry has one process, the medical industry has another. Both have extensive phone systems, long hold times and, mind numbing background music periodically interrupted by a voice "Your call is very important to us. Please continue to hold for the next available service representative." More often than not Chenko must leave a message. Both industries call this "service." Chenko takes the attitude "Cut the executive bonuses and put more people on the phones you cheap bastards!" Through Billy Kaloon he sets aside a financial reserve for the unexpected. He ignores what he can and pays off what he can't.

The will is in order, tax liabilities minimized, ownerships established, a reserve set aside. He made the calls, went to the meetings, got the signatures. All high-risk investments switched to stable certificates of deposit. For the time being the land deal is on the back burner.

The land with the pole barn is where he rebuilds and refinishes furniture from garage sales or Goodwill. Chenko treasures the place. He likes to buy a piece for twenty dollars, put twenty-five dollars into it and move it for one hundred fifty dollars. He never refers to the pieces as antiques, but never corrects a buyer if they use the term. This activity produces some customers, but more importantly an audience. Someone he knows will always drop in if they see Old Red parked outside. If there is a plus side his hesitation to sell the barn has increased his buyer's interest. Its sale will be one less headache for Ilene, but she will get ownership for now. Chenko is satisfied with the first phase. He's ready to move on to the second phase of his agenda, the visitations, conversations and conclusions.

The days are getting shorter and the temperature is dropping. The screens need to come down; the yard is filling up with leaves. Ilene wants to move some plants and have the gardens cut back. Old Red needs tires and a tune up.

There's a couch in the basement at Ilene's sister's (Margret) that needs to be moved from her place to a friend before the weather gets bad. All the activity autumn brings weigh on Chenko. He wonders if all will get done given his condition.

He begins to evaluate his condition. His appetite is weak, he's losing weight, he is always cold and tires easily, cuts and bruises take longer to heal. But he can still move and nothing hurts. The prescription helps. Or maybe it's the tablets from the health store, maybe both. Who knows? No need to change anything. With the exception of the weight, which he believes comes from nerves and eating more tablets than food, as opposed to his terminal illness, he attributes all his health problems to old age. How he feels is due more to age than illness, he rationalizes. He's only been told he's sick, but he knows he's old. For the most part Chenko feels if the sixties are the new forties, it isn't working for him.

On a clear cool night Chenko bundles up and sits on the deck after Ilene goes to bed. He's looking at the stars, trying to use them to map out a strategy for the second phase of his agenda. Out in space there has to be a star that will guide him. He's smoking, but it isn't a cigar. He wishes he had paper and pencil to write down all that is exploding in his mind, but is in no mood to get them. He'll remember. It's all so clear.

His head in a cloud of smoke Chenko's thoughts begin to wander. As he gazes at the star-filled sky the concept of space traps him. He reaches a conclusion that space cannot exist without time and distance. Space the distance between two points and the time needed to get from one point to the other. It's what marks a beginning and an end. Chenko takes another hit and thinks of the one-to-seven dog year scale he has set in his mind. At the top of the scale a star that takes seven years, or forty-nine dog years, to reach. He wonders if has enough engine power and sufficient fuel to land on the "seventh star." He thinks of his condition as a mission he never wanted.

Off in the distance the seven brightest stars against this dark background become family and friends who need to be visited, they're in a pattern that resembles an hour glass. He'll need a rocket to reach the seventh star in this constellation and begins to build one in his mind. It wouldn't be hard Chenko thinks, "Hell, I grew up in the space age," and wanders back to an early October in 1957, eight years old and in third grade when the crazy Russians put up Sputnik and won the war of thrust. Every morning when he got dressed for his day at General Grade School the news on the radio filled him in. "Still beeping...Still out there." It wasn't until sometime in January that the beeping, from the orbiting two-hundred-pound metal ball, stopped. Sputnik was up there almost all of that winter. It was a big deal.

At the time everyone was concerned with the race into outer space and the one thing Chenko heard over and over again was "We're behind!" The implication was the United States was in trouble. At eight or nine, Chenko was used to being in some type of trouble alone, now the whole country was in trouble. This was a different kind of trouble. No one was alone. It was collective in nature.

His lighter quits on him. He sighs as he gets up to find another. "Expect the unexpected. We were running out of time." The words reflect his condition in his subconscious. The situation then, something he can relate to now. His condition is his second Sputnik, as unexpected as Sputnik was back in 1957.

But as he remembers, James Van Allen and Werhner Von Braun and a bunch of other guys, in January of 1958 answer the Russians and thrust Explorer One into space, instrumentation by Van Allen and engine by Von Braun. Chenko laughs to himself as he wonders if they're the two V's behind the German V2 rocket, like he's solved some big mystery. He takes another hit and mutters, "We picked up a boy after the war too." He recalls the beeping that stopped the previous January returns the following January only this time it's our sound from outer space.

By the time he's in the fourth grade it seems the U.S. thrust problem is solved, but it isn't. From the fourth grade on the "space race," which is another term for "arms race" is on with the Reds, which is another term for Russians. A "Cold War" started by thrust. Everything on the globe turned to - us against them, Buffalo's and Bears. The Zachenko's were a little more concerned than others.

That same year, 1958, along with Explorer One, the U.S. also launched the Nautilus, the first atomic powered submarine. To Chenko this is a bigger deal. The sub went completely under the North Pole. The feat of going under the polar ice cap scares him more than going into outer space. He once had a small version of the Nautilus produced by Kellogg's and placed in boxes of Rice Krispies that at time let everyone know we not only had the skies covered, but oceans too. We could stay under water a long time and pop up anywhere. His Rice Krispies sub was powered by baking powder.

Chenko drifts in out of these thoughts. He laughs to himself, "We're all veterans of the Cold War, all the Boomers. Cold War Boomers." The thought comes to him he's in another Cold War. He tells himself "I'm okay with it. They last a long time" He smiles and lights another cigar, but only takes two or three hits, then flicks the cigar as far as he can out in the yard, the lit end like the flame from a rocket, while he exhales its exhaust.

For a moment he sees in his mind the perfect three stage rocket, liquid fuel not solid. It's exactly what he needs to visit the stars, each stage engineered to give the right amount of thrust for each phase of his agenda. Each capable of covering the time and distance needed. In the end he will be like a rocket that fades from sight and sends back a signal everything is okay. He gathers up his lighter and cigars, puts away the chair and takes the rocket to bed with him.

******

The following morning Chenko gets dressed, heads to the Y and swims. Showers, but doesn't shave. Heads home, takes his prescription, knocks back some tablets from the health store, and eats two pieces of peanut butter toast, an apple, orange and banana.

While eating he starts talking to his dog Lefty and the cats Morton, Al and Flossie. Morton stays, but Al and Flossie head for another room. He begins telling Lefty and Morton the dream he had about a three-stage rocket. He clarifies that the rocket came from a dream or a self-induced trance, he wasn't sure, but it didn't matter. He's always truthful with Lefty, Morton, Al and Flossie. The dog and three cats are the only beings he's talked about his condition, told them from day one, first chance he got. They all know.

Lefty is lying on the floor, her head over one paw and eyes open, wagging her tail occasionally. Morton sits cleaning himself with eyes closed acting like he's listening. Chenko goes into the design for the second phase. It will be built around the answers to three questions. Who will he visit? (First stage) What will he say during the visit? (Second stage) How will he conclude the visit (Third stage)? He throws these three questions out to the two pets as if they have the answer. He waits a few moments, wipes the apple on his shirt looks at Lefty and Morton, and determines if they have the answers, they're not talking.

He takes a bite from the apple and thinks about the first stage of this three-stage rocket he needs to launch the second phase of his agenda, the relationships. He tells the two "It's the biggest." He continues with "It can't be too big or it won't get off the ground." Outside of the family, who should know? Soon the dog and the cat are asleep and he has to answer his own questions: "A couple from school, a couple from the Army, a couple from work, a couple from the neighborhood? That would be eight. Too many, but six might work.". Chenko drops the Army. Any candidate from this group would be out of state and would be someone he'd like to see, but doesn't need to. It gets an honorable mention. Chenko decides that no more than six from outside the family need to know for different reasons. He is soon made aware of how many he has to choose from, it becomes a problem.

From the outset the plan for the second phase is to tell the family first. Should he tell them individually or as a group? He wrestles with the concepts as he moves on to the orange and begins to peel it. Chenko expresses all his thoughts out loud to his sleeping audience and gazes out the kitchen window at the colors of the leaves on the trees and throughout his yard. The sun is bright and the temperature warm. He pulls the orange apart and eats it in sections. The thought of how to tell the family is replaced by the urge to rake the yard and come back to the problem at hand. He tells the two slumbering pets "Might not get the answers today, but the yard will be done."

After eating the orange, he makes short work of the banana, it's gone in three bites. Chenko wipes his mouth with his right sleeve and makes his way to the deck. He opens the sliding glass door and leaves it open for Lefty and Morton then fires up a cigar. Soon Lefty joins him, but Morton stays inside. Al hears the sliding glass door open and joins Lefty. The two casually follow Chenko's voice to the garage and watch as he gets his gloves, rake and looks for the blue plastic tarp. He wrestles his way to the far left-corner and finds it loosely folded on a bottom shelf by the lawn mower, three shelves down from the missing satchel. On top of the tarp is a coiled fifty-foot orange extension cord. With a quick glance, he spots the open space on the third shelf in front of the satchel, moves the extension cord and grabs the tarp, deciding he'll rake the front first.

Lefty and Al follow him to the front yard and find a sunny place to lie down until his barely audible voice puts their eyes in a comfortable glaze. They're in the abstract place that precedes sleep, but Chenko thinks he has their undivided attention. "It's like the kid you don't want to fight on the playground, but have to," Chenko sighs and returns to the problem of how tell the family. "You know the kid will absolutely kick your ass. But hey! You have to show up." He begins to rake the yard and tell the dog and cat how life is like the playground full of comedy and tragedy. He remembers Donnie Fisher. Donnie and his silver lighter, lighting everyone's smokes, he never smoked, but loved carrying it, made him feel like everyone else.

He's amused by the thought, the fact that Donnie will never be a candidate, one of the bright far-off stars that has to be visited, but that doesn't stop Chenko from thinking about him. Donnie was another one from the basement of General. No one tried harder on every level than Donnie, no one on every level got as short changed as Donnie. His cards were always bad and if he's an angel, it makes Chenko think twice about becoming one. He rakes a pile onto the tarp and wonders if Donnie is even alive.

For some reason Donnie won't leave him. If this isn't enough, Donnie brings to mind Gabriel Gandacinni, "Gandy." The thought brings a smile. Gandy hired Chenko the summer he graduated from high school, the summer before Ohio State. He had a tree service and landscaping business, enough work to keep sixteen guys like Chenko busy for a summer. He had residential and city business and it was hard to get on a crew. If a kid got on one, they found he expected more than anyone could give, could take abuse to an art form, but paid well. Working for Gandy was like being part of a highly dysfunctional family, but family just the same. Aside from all his sarcasm and abuse he had a quality about him, that one couldn't put their finger on, that in the end made one love him. Both employees and customers knew he was a fair man. Only the employees, unlike the customers, knew he was crazy. Gandy would certainly be one of the bright stars Chenko would want hit with his rocket, but died soon after Chenko got out of the Army. Chenko tells Lefty and Al. "Gandy already knows."

Gandy had a brick shop with a huge bay. At the rear of the shop was an office with two huge glass windows. Inside, chairs, two desks and a bunch of filing cabinets, all the paper work that was supposed to be in their drawers, on top of them. For the most part the drawers were empty. Tony Bonalli ran the office, he could find anything in that office within seconds, and he also was the "good cop" in the "good cop/bad cop" management style Gandy used.

The bay held every tool needed to carry out the business venture. The yard was three acres with a half-acre dirt and oil parking lot. Parked on it was a double-axle stake truck, a chipper, a bucket truck and three, three-quarter ton pick-ups. The tools and trucks were always in good condition. This is because Gandy always accused the last person to use a tool or a truck of total misapplication, it was miracle whatever one had used still worked. These conversations were inevitable. Everyone learned to take care of what they used to keep these conversations as short as possible.

The first democracy Chenko participated in was in that shop and yard. Aside from Gandy's unpredictable behavior was his nature. He hired both Jocks and Hoods along with one village idiot, Donnie. Everyone got a chance with Gandy. The early part of the summer each group walked around like cats and dogs hissing and growling, occasionally taking a swipe or snap at one another. Donnie was in the middle, accepted by both groups for what he was and never involved. By the end of the summer both groups groomed each other and shared one common interest, Gandy, warning one another whenever he was in the area. The two packs become one because of their common fear of a predator. The shared self-preservation breeds friendships on both sides in a very short time; for the most part all learn to work together, put their differences aside.

No one escaped the derogatory nickname Gandy would give each and what he would call them all season long. Everyone started out like Alex Haley's "Kunta Kinte" in *Roots* and became "Toby" by the end of the summer. Over time every employee answered to the name given them. Jack Warman, who'd done some weekends in jail before Gandy hired him, became "Felon." Chenko because he was going to college was dubbed "College Boy." There were others "Spit," "Piss," "Bag," "Dent," "Fat Pants," "Shrimp Dick." Chenko, if he thought about it long enough, could probably recall everyone's nickname, but Donnie was always "Donnie." He was the only one to escape this and that was fair.

Chenko pulls a load of leaves on the tarp to the back yard and dumps them in the area Ilene has set aside for such material. A few moments after the work are done Lefty and Al show up. Chenko scratches his left forearm on the rose bush coming out of the area and reacts with a "Damn It!" Lefty and Al jump away from him. For an instant he thinks of tearing the bush out. "Already got my leg," he tells the two. He comes to his senses when he thinks of Ilene and instead decides to take a short break and have a beer and a smoke.

Lefty and Al follow him to the kitchen and are given a treat for being such a good audience. Lefty follows Chenko back to the deck and Al yawns after his treat and leisurely follows. Chenko begins to close the sliding glass door on him as he stands between deck and kitchen to help Al in his decision. Al knows Chenko isn't going to wait and talk to him like Ilene and is forced to jump on to the deck or get hit by the door, knows it doesn't matter to Chenko. It annoys him. He doesn't like being rushed. He gives Chenko the look.

Chenko takes a long pull from his beer and sees "Lump," Wayne Tabor. He tells Lefty and Al "Lump didn't get his name from Gandy, but from the crews. No one could stand him." He was one of Gandy's crew chiefs; his crew did all the city work. Guys wanted to get on Harlan's crew and do residential. Harlan was like Tony, normal.

Lump, on the other hand, was a living example of everything bad about a severely under-educated redneck ridge-running hill-jack, straight from hell. Since he didn't have any minorities to push around, as soon as Gandy was out of sight, Lump would start in on Donnie, the only guy dumber than Lump. He used Donnie to let them all know Donnie was someone you didn't want to be. That he owned Donnie, owned them. He was a prick.

Lump was about seven years older than the rest of the crew, twenty-five or six. Brainless and toothless. Rumor was he missed the draft because all his teeth had rotted out; he had full upper and lower false teeth. Nothing could be done about the brain; he was so messed up the Army didn't even want him. He was wiry and deceptively strong for his size. He was mean as a snake, worked his crew hard, but did not lead by example. Lump spent a lot of time in the truck. That's how he got his name: the "Lump in the truck."

He held the "Gandy card" and challenged anyone of them to tell Gandy how he treated Donnie; always leaving the impression he'd win that contest, always reminding his crew "I'm Gandy's right-hand man...you piece of shit." This was something to think about, as bad as he was, in the scheme of things, for whatever reason, Lump was a "made man."

To cover himself at the end of the day he'd slap everyone on the back and act friendly, offering to buy pops from the machine next to the office. It was all an act for Gandy, who had his doubts about Wayne. It soon became the practice, that first, you never called Wayne "Lump" at the shop even though Gandy knew Wayne's nickname. It was one he hadn't given and even though it was correct, reflected badly on his choice for a crew chief. It brought out his stubborn side. He didn't need to be reminded. If there was a problem with Wayne, he'd settle it his own way. He didn't need any help. Second, you never accepted a pop from Lump to reinforce Gandy's doubts. The Jocks and Hoods on both crews followed these two rules religiously. However, it was acceptable among all to have Lump buy you a pop and give it to Donnie, but the act was sure to bring repercussions.

The Felon and Fat Pants have both been beaten down by Lump on one job or another for coming to Donnie's defense. Lump had to be pulled off of them. Everyone got a week with Harlan then a week with Lump. Any day you had to go out with Lump was a bad day. When Chenko's turn came Gandy was on vacation. That's why it took place by the pop machine. Chenko is standing by it thinking how Lump gets Donnie to cry at lunch, taking his lighter, blowing smoke and flicking his ashes in his face, tripping him when he moves away. Someone was going after Lump that day. It turns out to be Chenko. He is the most agitated.

Lump knows this and makes him the target of his standard end of the day offer. Chenko tells him to stick it up his ass. Lump tells Chenko there's a big parking lot outside and to bring the bottle that just rattled its way through the machine with him, to see whose ass it's going up. He then takes out his teeth, just like he did with the Felon and Fat Pants. Wraps them up in a filthy handkerchief, puts them in his pocket, knowing no one is going to hold them. Chenko grabs the bottle and hands it to Donnie.

Lefty and Al are told how everyone files out to the lot and watches Lump beat Chenko senseless. The only reason Lump stops is because he becomes worried about breaking his hands. But Chenko gets some shots in and never quits. What is strange about it, Chenko tells Lefty and Al, is from that day on he begins to crowd Lump every chance he gets. Others try to remind him of the beating and all Chenko tells them is "He got to me early. Next time will be different." His attitude spooks Lump.

Chenko knows Lump remembers one or two shots. It isn't too long and others begin to crowd Lump at times telling Lump they're getting "Chenko's disease." Later on, because of Chenko the Felon and Fat Pants even the score with Lump. After Fat Pants, Lump missed a day of work. On more than one occasion after the parking lot, Chenko would give Lump the crazy smile and in a low voice through clenched teeth would tell Lump, "Let's go. You and me, you mother-fucking hill-jack." He did it at random times with no provocation in front of everyone just to see what would happen. Lump never took him up on the offer. Even if it turned out the same, Lump knew the Felon and Fat Pants would be in the wings. Gandy let it all play out. The next summer Wayne Tabor was gone.

Chenko swallows the last of the beer and flicks his cigar out in the backyard that is still full of leaves, unconcerned about any fire it could start. He's done it more than once and never started a fire. It didn't make it right, there was always a chance, but Chenko didn't worry about it, just like after a while he didn't worry about Wayne Tabor. He gets up from his chair and stretches, telling Lefty and Al, "I'll finish up the yard now." Tells the two it was clear to him why Donnie and the rest of them showed up. "Let's go, you and me, you mother-fucking disease."

******

As he takes the screens down and cuts the gardens back, Chenko runs a list of people through his mind trying to build the booster stage to launch the second phase. Every day he has a design that will be replaced the following day by a new design. Someone he doesn't' think of will surface causing the change, each with their reason for consideration. The family still comes first, end of subject. But he knows each new design to take in those outside the family is really a stalling tactic to keep from doing what first needs to be done, tell the family. He wants to escape, but can't, they have to be told. It frustrates Chenko. He begins to think who he tells might not be as important as the second stage of the rocket, what he will tell them. The solution to the problem might be found in building the second stage before the first stage.

Chenko ponders the tactic. He forces himself back to the family, wife, children, brothers and sister. Ezra and Helene already know. He starts with Ilene, running some opening lines through his mind and begins to realize he doesn't have the poetry to take away the agony. "I didn't spend forty years in the wilderness with you," he rehearses. "You've always been my promised land." He shakes his head, files the lines in the back of his mind.

No matter what he says, Chenko knows her reaction will be one of anger, resolution and compassion. At least this is what he anticipates as the firing order of the engine behind this rocket. Anger over all his bad habits she tried to break over the years, but failed. Resolution when she balances the good and the bad. Compassion, hopefully, from the good outweighing the bad. He ponders this order for a while. The firing could just as well run in reverse: compassion, resolution and anger. Anger would be the worst last stage. He realizes he'll have to pick his words carefully to get the right firing order.

Another thought comes. There's also the possibility that the "end" he's going to have to bring up in the beginning, might be taken as the end of the marriage as opposed to the end of life. When he makes the clarification, it will be worse than what is first expected. Either one is bad. She might be mad enough to consider the first in response to the clarification. How to approach the "end" is more difficult than he first thought. If he doesn't do this right the situation could end in an explosion on the launch pad. If he doesn't get the words right, he won't fade out into space like a well launched rocket, the end Chenko wants.

All the thoughts of telling Ilene, let alone the kids, brothers, sister, run together creating a huge traffic jam in his mind. Chenko looks for an exit and finds it by thinking again of those outside the family. He could practice on them. It wouldn't matter if he messed up. He'll learn from them what to tell his wife and kids, brothers and sisters. He takes the detour.

******

As he walks to the mailbox one mid-November morning, it's warm, but raining. The rain knocks the remaining leaves to the ground, the trees are now bare and he bets the following day will be cold. Except for the Army he's lived his whole life in Ohio; he knows how the weather this time of the year can bounce around. Northeast Ohio, about fifty miles south of Lake Erie, to be exact, can have snow, ice, slush, and mind numbing cold. He knows about the "lake effect." He'll talk winters with anyone from Wisconsin, Minnesota, Pennsylvania, New York, New England, or any other state that has a cold spell of three or more months. The toughest months on the schedule are right around the corner, December, January and February. Winter isn't his favorite season, but Chenko is okay with it, he sure missed it when he was out of the country, in the tropics, on government business in Southeast Asia.

The mail is gathered and he walks slowly, sorting through it. The initial sort shows one magazine and eight pieces of mail. A quarter of the mail is solicitations from charities, half, solicitations to invest, an eighth a bill, another eighth, personal for Ilene, even though his name may appear next to hers on the envelope. Chenko hasn't received a personal letter addressed just to him in years. He's okay with that too; the last one was enough. He always feels a sense of relief when he sees he has no personal mail.

More importantly, the day's mail doesn't include any from the medical or insurance industries. Over the past weeks or dog months, the mailbox has only fed Chenko's cynicism; he feels his illness feeds these industries. For them to find a cure is to lose a food source. They're both predators. By the time he reaches the garage he's smiling because this day he doesn't have to deal with his cynicism, but knows, like the weather, this could change tomorrow.

By the time he puts the mail on the new granite kitchen counter he thinks about moving some plants for Ilene. But he could get a pass, it is raining. He decides to go the barn and work on a dresser he bought at the end of summer. Maybe start a fire in the pot belly stove with seventy-five percent of the day's mail, not for warmth, but practice for what's around the corner. He makes his way to the garage, simultaneously fires up Old Red and a cigar and heads that way.

Old Red rolls down the gravel drive leading to the barn. "There he is!" he grumbles. Chenko is referring to the Blue Jay hanging around the big sycamore tree next to the barn. "Always bugging the other birds, always shooting off its mouth, I'm going to get that son-of-bitch," and flicks his cigar from the window. The feud with the jay started in the spring when Chenko threw a rock at the bird and just missed its head, but hit the tailgate of Old Red, leaving a nice dent. He has an alternate parking spot now whenever he spots the jay, where the truck is always behind him.

Over the summer the contest has developed a set of rules. He won't use the .22 he has in the barn. The jay has to be killed with a rock to be fair. Chenko gets out and combs the gravel for about a one to one-and-one-half inch cube of stone, finds it and moves into range. Optimum range is about twenty-five feet to line drive the perfect shot at the jay sitting on a branch fifteen feet off the ground. It will be like getting hit by a boulder. He'll have to move quietly another twenty-five feet to be in optimum range. As Chenko moves into range he senses the jay ready to take off and rushes his throw from about thirty feet out and misses by about four feet. To date, this shot is the closest. The jay takes off swearing at him. He gives it the finger, thinking of upping the ante and getting a sling-shot.

The man-door is opened and Chenko enters his realm. The first thing he passes is his Sportster, it's a 1200, a rare metal flake green, three-point-three-gallon tank, 2002 Harley Davidson HDL stock Sportster "Sport" to be exact. It's his most recent acquisition; Chenko bought it when he retired four years ago. Ilene okayed it, "You never got one like I thought you would when the kids were young. Go ahead." He walks past the bike toward the work benches he built and the tools he's acquired over the years. Under the green steel roof that covers his sixty-one by thirty-two-foot building are the walls, hanging on them the street signs he couldn't pass up in his youth.

The head of an eight-point buck is over the first set of double doors, twelve points over second set. He didn't bag the deer. He isn't a hunter. All he can tell visitors about them is they belong to some friends. In fact, half of all that decorates Chenko's walls are from buddies, all the stuff unacceptable for even the basement or garage at their homes. The stuff their wives told them is unfit and isn't staying, now hangs in Chenko's barn. Most of what is on the walls is the off color and insulting items he and his buddies couldn't resist picking up in their travels. The best description of the place comes from Ilene, who told him once

"It's like walking through your head." His daughter Hope described it as "The place where junk comes to die."

Chenko walks to the refrigerator, opens the freezer door, pulls out a bottle of George Dickel and pours a shot. He puts the bottle back and closes the door. He gulps the shot down, grimaces, and laughs at the bumper sticker on the freezer door. *"Consciousness – That Confusing Time between Naps."* He nods his approval like it's the first time he's ever read it. He walks to the stove and throws his Dixie cup along with the days solicitations into it, soaks them with starter fluid, adds some cardboard from dead twelve packs, adds some kindling, a couple logs and gives the pile a final soaking. He stands back about two feet, lights a cigar then throws the match through the cast iron door. The flames shoot out the about two feet and quickly settle down.

He heads over to the dresser and begins to briefly inspect it. He got it at a garage sale in Canton for twenty bucks. It's a piece from the late twenties or early thirties. It's beat up, but has some nice inlay. The veneer is about an eighth of an inch thick; the five drawers are dove-tailed. Other than the right rear corner leg that has to be rebuilt, it's a piece that could be brought back in about a month. For a moment Chenko thinks about the time in dog years and it scares him.

It's a short walk to his office. He built his office. It's a smaller version of Gandy's; instead of windows to give a view of the floor, he has a big old wooden four pane glass storm door, all wood and glass, made in the Forties. It's nice and he did a good job setting it. Inside he has some old rear-view mirrors attached to the corners and trained on the door. From inside ninety percent of the floor is in view. Like

Gandy's, everything that should be in his desk is on his desk, the couch and two chairs. The walls in the office are covered with the same type of nonsense as the walls out on the floor. It's well-lit and in the winter warms up fast when the small space heater is plugged in. There's a window in front of his desk, it gives the view of a field and some woods.

On the desk is a box Chenko made out of walnut, its dimensions the same as a White Owl Cigarillo cigar box. He took his time when he made it, did it right. It's a nice box, has a false bottom that holds the things he gets from people like Jimmy Chesterfield. Chenko reaches for it. Lifts some molding to unlock the false bottom, pulls it open, grabs a bag and some papers and rolls a small joint. His plan is to take no more than three hits and put the roach back in the box, he takes five.

Chenko sits at his desk and thinks of all the people he's thought of during the second phase, their faces passing in review. There's paper and pen within easy reach and for a moment considers making a list, but instead leans back in his chair. The list is replaced by the thought of who will show up today. He sits, reminded of the old Akron bus station waiting for someone to come in. After a few moments he gets up and walks to the dresser like one walk to a vending machine, something to do while waiting for the bus to pull in.

He inspects the front of the dresser. There are five drawers and he selects the third one. He pulls it completely out of the dresser and examines the outside bottom of the drawer. Branded in the center is a worn logo, the only words he can make out "Birmingham, Alabama." He pulls the two above and below it to see if they're branded, only the center drawer is branded. As he slides the drawers back in, he thinks of Birmingham, Alabama, as a place he's been, and that he knows someone who grew up there. The bus has just pulled in.

There's a box of tools that holds rasps, files, knives, scrapers and sand paper on the workbench between the two sets of double doors. Chenko places it on the dresser trying to decide if he wants to remove the finish or fix the leg. He decides the leg. Walks over to the bench by the door and gets the box holding the cat's paw, claw hammer, razor saw, and chisels. While he gathers all the tools he'll need at the job site, he's still lost in Birmingham, Alabama until Roosevelt "Zoom" Brown, who grew up there, gets off the bus and Chenko smiles. He comes to mind, out of nowhere, like Donnie.

He worked a one hundred-twenty days rubber strike in 1976 with Zoom. The two of them spliced four-and-a-half inch I D (Inside Diameter) by six hundred sixty-foot lengths of irrigation hose sent in by customers for repair. They were the Anaconda of hose, powering giant lawn sprinklers through the peach and orange orchards primarily down south and out west. A length costs around four thousand dollars. They worked the third shift six days a week splicing hose. At least twice a week they worked the third and first shift, only on the first shift they drove forklifts to the loading docks, emptying trash bins in long bed stake trailers hooked to semis. Once a truck pulled away with Chenko still on the trailer. Chenko shocked the driver when he appeared out nowhere in the driver's side window a mile and half down the road. But for the most part it's just the two of them in their own corner of the fifth floor in an ancient factory operated by the Industrial Products Division, splicing hose.

Chenko worked over thirty years for a Fortune 500 Company in the rubber game. He was an analyst, a-mid level job in the organization. When he began, five big rubber companies stood in Akron. In the space of thirty-two years and some change, to be exact, at the end of his career, only one remained, thinner and weaker than when he began his career with them. He worked seven years in Industrial Products, a non-core business, and twenty-five years in Tire Production and Planning, the core business.

During his career he dealt with an army of consultants, when that was the fad, hordes of MBA's, watched a tire company build a pipeline that went nowhere, soldiered through a take-over attempt, survived countless managers, directors, and vice presidents, went through seven CEO's. Some of the executives were good; most were bad, always cutting workers instead of their bonus. Even in the worst of times they *managed* to get their bonus. Seems that's all they managed. It was a place that held onto a feudal culture in which the Dukes and Earls were given democratic titles, Presidents, Vice Presidents, a place in reality that has a king, a court of his choosing, and a ton of serfs they liked to call "associates," who live at their mercy. It's not a place for the faint of heart or thin skinned. Chenko always refers to company as the "rubber shop."

In the second year of his career Chenko crossed a picket line six days a week for four months, so did Zoom. Both were taken from office to factory, from suits to coveralls, thanks to the United Rubber Workers. Chenko crossed the line at six foot and one hundred eighty-five pounds, Zoom at six foot four and two hundred thirty-five pounds. Zoom was a former tight end for Kentucky. When Chenko found out from co-workers, he told Zoom, "I never heard of a tight end ever being called 'Zoom.' "I'd run your ass down," Zoom laughing. "What ya going to do once ya get there, "Bounce?" And so Chenko picked up another nickname.

He was a year older than Chenko. Zoom only worked for the company three years and then went with a distributor in Detroit, but while he was in Akron he and Chenko became good friends. At the end of the third shift in those days both could always be found in the Rosebud Tavern drinking the whiskey sours and mint juleps they usually would never drink around others. Zoom and Bounce become regulars and generally the only two early morning customers, salt and pepper sitting at the end of the bar, straightening out the problems of the world.

They didn't have any trouble learning their differences when they first met. Chenko grew up around white guys, Zoom black guys. Each knew the derogatory epithets each group had for the other, the myths and the distrust. Both bridged it. Both knew guys on the picket line and Chenko and Zoom were the kind of guys who were teased instead of harassed when they crossed it. Chenko told Zoom he liked crossing the line with him. "You're such a big target, draw a lot of boys," Zoom laughing and replying, "I'll get you down field…"

They used their size and age difference to joke with each other instead of the color of their skin when they wanted to get something going. It was good, they both became color blind in the competitions they'd have with each other, both were .500 in the mental and physical events they entered into with each other to make the third shift fly by. One is faster, the other stronger, one is intuitive, the other perceptive.

After about forty-five days the boys on the picket line are getting a little surly, start fires in fifty-five gallon drums, have quit shaving and become more intimidating. Both get into the practice in which the first to arrive in the parking lot waits for the other. Sometimes Chenko and Zoom would smoke in the parking lot, sizing up the picketers before approaching the line. Zoom went through Bull Conner and his attack dogs, the Birmingham Bus Boycott; he didn't miss much of the Civil Rights strife growing up in Alabama. Chenko survived the Tet in Viet Nam. Both know this about the other, but don't talk about it much. Their prior experiences make the line small change in comparison, but both know it wouldn't take much to get things going the wrong way. Their past experiences help them.

Zoom tells Chenko in a sympathetic breath, "They getting thin." Chenko answers in a realistic breath "Five white, two black, six empties by the fire... you ready for the "Wigger/Nigger treatment tonight?" They already know what to expect. Zoom smiles at the hidden irony; they flick their smokes in a puddle and cross the street. That was as rough as it got. The white and black guys on the line each throw out their own racial epithet at Chenko and Zoom, the two of them occasionally, whispering to the other, "Whoa! That's a new one to me."

Once inside they'd wrestle the five by four-foot-tall reels of hose over to a table, run an iron bar through the center and with chain hoist lift the reel off the floor. One would steady the reel as the other took the end over the table to a mounted empty reel, set the end in the reel axle and begin to manually crank until they found what needed to be spliced. They alternated the steadying and pulling, and if there were any complaints they were directed at the company, not each other. It was an all-manual process, and both would talk about how nice it would be to have a motor on the hoist and the wind up. Chenko muttered, "It's like they don't know about electricity," Zoom replied, "Lotta things the company don't know 'bout, Bounce."

Dickie Pontey is an industrial engineer about five years older than Chenko, a fair-haired boy, who has a sponsor on executive row, he puts out a robust number of eight splices a shift, a number never achieved when the union did the splices. Their average was seven. Each splice requires eight steps and a fifty-minute cure time. Dickie wrote the procedure. Chenko and Zoom are always at war with him, telling him when they never hit his number to get them a forklift and some motors. Dickie completely ignores their request. They always refer to him as "Dick the Prick." He works with them one night and they get three splices. He only does this once. The experience, however, isn't enough to get him to change his number. He brags to upper management how he went down and showed both how to do it. The implication being the problem isn't the process, but the people.

After about the second week Chenko and Zoom have played around with the process enough where they could do eight. Each discusses the splicing procedure with the other like surgeons as they operate on the injured. Together they are able to take three steps out of the process and reduce curing time by fifteen minutes by increasing the temperature and reducing the pressure. In the following weeks they increase their output gradually, leveling out at seven by the end of the first month.

Actually, both could get nine splices if they wanted to, but both agreed there's no point in furthering Dickie's career, future rubber generations would thank them, or breaking the union rate in fairness to the boys on the line. They're comfortable at seven. Their number. Of all their splices only four fail the hydro pressure test. Each received a letter of appreciation, like everyone, signed by Dickie when the strike ends. They never bother to tell anyone of the changes they made in the process that would only open a can of worms with Dickie. They're satisfied there are still "Lotta things the company don't know 'bout"... and put that card in their back pocket.

Chenko reaches for the cat's paw, after putting the dresser on its side to work on the leg. Each step he takes to repair the dresser becomes longer and longer as he recalls his days with Zoom. Most of this time is being spent looking at the job and thinking of Zoom. The end came about a year or two after the strike. After the strike they ran into each other occasionally at work. Sometimes one would make up a reason to be other's area just to visit. Other than this nothing changes, around the holidays they make time to hit the Rosebud.

Zoom was there the day the "yellow shirt incident" took place by the coffee machine on the second floor of the factory where the offices were located. Chenko set it up wanting some advice. Chenko had a new boss Rod Wealthy. His first directive upon taking over the Marketing Department, including Chenko and seven others, is informing every one of his dislikes of any dress shirt that isn't white or blue, especially yellow. He never gives directives on the business, just appearance. Appearance is, the only thing he knows. Because this is all he knows, it soon becomes apparent he's not shy when it comes to throwing someone under the bus to make it appear he's handling a problem.

"Mr. Wealthy" as he liked to be called, has been in power six months when the incident takes place. On Fridays in the fall on just about every phone there's a bookie sheet. One of the unwritten perks of being on the second floor is filling out sheets on pro and college football. For the first two hours of the day only the phones get answered. During this time most gather around the vending machine areas, groups come and go, everything has to be discussed. The activity is authorized by the fact that someone in power is letting the sheets happen. Then one day the sheet is replaced by a letter informing all they'd be fired if found with one and all know someone has fallen from power.

The Friday of the incident Mr. Wealthy sees his department by the vending machines, decides to try to be one of the boys and get a cup of coffee. His white and blue policy over the months is watered down by pin-stripes and Tattersall, but no yellow. Chenko who received a pale-yellow broad cloth dress shirt as a gift from an old girlfriend, has it on, never giving the white and blue policy any thought when he got dressed that day. Mr. Wealthy takes note and waits for the right moment to pounce and demonstrate he wasn't kidding about yellow shirts. While he waits, he tries to joke with the boys who only acknowledge his remarks with nods, not words, and go back to their own conversations. Everyone knows he doesn't fit in. But each is respectful the less said to the boss the better.

When the pause Mr. Wealthy is waiting for comes, he begins staring at Chenko until everyone notices, extending the pause. In the protracted silence Chenko begins to stare back, wondering what is up, never thinking of his shirt. Mr. Wealthy finally speaks, "Zachenko, where you going today in that shirt, a pig fucking contest?" It catches all by surprise.

The group is hushed waiting for the reply. It's the playground Chenko thinks, he's going to make me an example to others, and in true form decides to go down swinging. He gives Mr. Wealthy a nod and smile. "As a matter of fact, I am. Understand you're a contestant."

Those who chose to take a sip of coffee at the time never got to swallow, turning the liquid into a mist shooting from their mouths when they hear his answer.

It was brazened, but well received, Mr. Wealthy smart enough to know it wouldn't be to his benefit to push back. He replied with, an artificial laugh, that let all know he'll pick the time and place to get his pound of flesh. He starts back to his office. Zoom got the second spray of the day. Mr. Wealthy still within earshot, in act of solidary for his friend, Zoom adds, "Man I feel sorry for that pig!" They'd go down together.

Within the year Chenko was laid off for almost a hundred days, a temporary lay-off, Mr. Wealthy tried for a permanent; Zoom gets cornered on his remark and decides to take an offer from Detroit, the only thing to remain the same, their friendship. Over the years both survive the career ending incident. Back in the barn, Chenko has a revelation of some of the things he has survived.

******

The following day Chenko heads to Akron to pick up a bench grinder he found on the internet. A body shop going out of business off Perkins, right before the bridge, has what he's been looking for; he recently burned up his grinder. He needs one for the dresser. Grinders are like pencil sharpeners in Chenko's shop and chisels like pencils. He likes to work an edge, likes watching the sparks fly. In truth he knows sharpening his tools is often another stalling tactic to avoid a task that needs to be done.

He gets off at Perkins. The light at the end of the exit ramp turns green; standing on the corner is a man holding a cardboard sign "HOMELESS – NEED HELP." The traffic moves slowly by him, no windows come down. Chenko is in the outside lane of the two lanes that allow the left hand turn and as he gets closer to the corner, he begins whisper to himself, "Donnie?" He rolls down the window as fast as he can and the whisper turns into a shout: "Donnie!"

At first, the man on the corner looks like some worn soldier just pulled a bad engagement, torn field jacket, faded and stained dark pants tucked in some beat-up canvas boots that are laced, but not tied. There's no hand at the bottom of the left sleeve. The man's eyes are hollow and he's mastered the blank stare. The sign hanging from his neck letting all know he's been tagged for special attention, no longer able to verbally describe the condition he's in; the sign could've just as easily read "WOUNDED – NEED CARE."

As Chenko gets closer the man's appearance begins to change. There's no way he can get to the inside lane for a closer look. As he gets closer the man's appearance improves. Chenko brings the outside lane to a crawl as he rounds the corner and shouts again: "Donnie!" The man searches for the voice and finds Chenko. Their eyes fill with recognition and recollection; both know the blue and brown eyes they've fixed on each other, both fill with excitement. The man waves, Chenko for a second sees the sign change again, asking "WHERE – YOU BEEN?"

As loud as he can Chenko yells: "Be right back!" He races to the first light, turns left, finds Market, goes right for a block and right again back to Perkins. Fortunately, the police are not in the area. The whole time he repeats, "It's Donnie!" In the space of five minutes, leaving the exit ramp and returning to it, Chenko begins to evaluate the situation. Doubt sets in and changes to "No way!"

He repeats it over and over. The only thought that convinces him there's a good chance it is Donnie, is that Donnie is left-handed and from what he had just seen it would just figure, somewhere along the line he lost it.

The ramp comes in full view, but there's no Donnie. He almost stops traffic as he drives by the ramp and then starts checking the streets and every alley. Finally, he pulls into a parking lot and again looks in all directions. His first thought "I gotta stay out of that box!" Then he can't decide if he really did see Donnie. He worries his doubt towards the end killed any chance.

After a few minutes Chenko starts Old Red, pulls out onto Perkins. It isn't long before he finds the body shop. There a man stands with his back to him locking the door, tired of waiting. Chenko, still dazed, gets out of the truck. When the man turns around, they recognize each other. They stare for a few moments and begin to laugh - "Chenko - you son of a bitch!" Jack Warman shouts. Chenko replies "The Felon! You're still alive?"

The Felon unlocks the door. "If it were anyone else today," the Felon tells Chenko. Both take a long stroll down memory lane. They have a few beers and laughs, Chenko tells the Felon about Donnie. The Felon gives him the look and tells Chenko, "He's dead, been dead awhile, calling hours were about ten years back..." Chenko nods and doesn't say any more about it.

On the way home, he thinks of all that has happened, Donnie, the Felon, and looks at every black man his age he passes for Zoom. By the time he gets home his thoughts have drifted. The first phase of his agenda had been handled by this time. The second phase of his agenda is not even close to being completed. The only ones who know are one dog and three cats. It bothers him. He's unaware of two things: First, all the people who have passed in review over the past weeks, or dog months, already know. Second, the first person he needs to tell is himself. Because of this the second phase of who he will visit, what he will tell them, how he'll conclude becomes an ongoing phase. The answers to all his questions are still out in space.

CHAPTER III: ATMOSPHERE

As Chenko wrestles with the second phase the atmosphere changes, the air is getting thinner, even though he hasn't gained any altitude in his unwanted mission. He takes his drugs and tablets, eats right and exercises which is becoming harder. There's a dull ache in his lower back, not in the center, but to the left. Chenko hesitates to put his hand on the area in fear of what he might find, but so far, he feels nothing. It's new and more a nuisance pain than a severe pain. His balance is good, but his pace is slow.

More than once Ilene has observed "You look tired Nye." Chenko sometimes answers... "I am," other times he lies. "I'm fine." The procedure he took over in handling his condition has left him with an appearance of just coming down with something or just getting over something. He's at mid-point on a scale ready to lean one way or the other. Chenko is trying to get the scale of fate to lean his way as if the situation he's in is a balancing act.

The couch at Margret's has been moved. The rain is changing to snow, and the thermostats turned up. Old Red still needs a tune-up and tires. Chenko takes a morning to line it up with his mechanic, Teddy, for the end of the month, wants it done before December. Teddy always takes care of Old Red, but it's not one of his favorite jobs, he tries to put it off for as long as possible even though the money is good. Two out of five times Teddy will find a problem he's never seen before while working on Chenko's truck. He is always asking Chenko "How's something like this happen?" Chenko always replies "Shouldn't I be asking that?" The appointment made Chenko heads to the barn.

The dresser is finished and Chenko sits in his realm and waits for a man named Linwood Sharltin. Chenko met him at an art festival in the Cuyahoga Valley two or three years back. At that show Chenko brought a roll-top desk he built from the dimensions given in a 1908 Sears catalog. The advertisement was long, typical of the time, and gave the full dimensions for pedestals, drawers, pigeon holes, gave its length, width and height. He made it out of mahogany pallets he got from the rubber shop. The nail holes and marks on the reclaimed wood after planer and finish give the desk an antique look, but it's a counterfeit. The work impresses Linwood, an antique dealer, who likes to work consignment deals.

Chenko knows him as a dealer, but Linwood is many things to many people, as Chenko soon discovers. The first meeting at the show set the table. Linwood wants to buy the desk. In a rare moment of conscience in their dealings over the desk, Chenko admits "It's not an *antique*," more than once. Linwood chooses not to hear this, telling Chenko more than once "Old *antique* desk like this would bring a lot of money." Chenko reaches two conclusions; first, Linwood is someone who just hears what he wants to hear. Second, what Linwood thinks is a lot of money isn't close to what Chenko thinks is a lot of money.

The desk is priced at $1,500 and somehow Linwood thinks he should be in the deal for at least $500, after his cash offer of $750 is rejected in one word: "Nope." He then offers some convoluted consignment deal Chenko laughs off. Chenko enjoys the slippery side of Linwood. The two develop a strange relationship in which Linwood is a man of many words and Chenko is a man of few, Linwood is complimentary, Chenko is blunt. They have little in common, but are somehow drawn to each other.

On the last day of the show the desk sells. Linwood comes by again and tells Chenko he told the Lord to send a customer to him. It's a goodwill gesture, and a sign, he then gives Chenko his card as if it were some type of award. Chenko takes the card and smiles, saying nothing, never mentioning the fact his name or the Lord's didn't come up once during the sale. Linwood leaves Chenko with a prophetic "Be seeing you."

This eventually comes to pass. Chenko found Linwood's card on his desk and wants the dresser out of the shop, wants to get another piece, a bigger piece for the next project. Linwood could inventory this dresser for him. Chenko is willing to work a consignment deal now. Consignments are the cold war of sales. As he waits, he won't be going anywhere until the dresser is sold. It becomes like the satchel; he won't be going anywhere until it's found. He's building a case, the satchel and now the dresser become part of the many reasons he needs more time, values for his equation for more time. Somehow, he's going to buy some additional time from Linwood. This is what the deal is really about.

Chenko ponders the magical box on his desk, but decides on a shot of Dickel. As he lights a cigar, throwing the match in the stove and the flames shoot out, a rusted-out pale blue 1976 American Motors Pacer rambles by the window pulling a small trailer. He does a double take watching it roll to a stop in the spot reserved for the blue jay. Chenko can't barely remember the last time he saw a Pacer. The car had a short life on the market; it came and went with the leisure suit. For a moment Chenko is impressed, it's a great car for one who deals in antiques, certainly got his attention. Linwood gets out wearing a pale green leisure suit and Chenko begins to wonder if he isn't imagining the whole scene. It's spooky. He takes a moment assuring himself he didn't visit the box.

Standing by a window, out of Linwood's view, he watches him make his way to the man-door, after first going to both sets of double doors. His mannerisms are unable to camouflage the impression of checking the double doors rather than an attempt to enter by them. Chenko wonders if he'll knock. He doesn't. Linwood opens the door slowly and he enters like *a thief in the night* hoping no one's home, taking inventory before looking for the owner.

When he sees Chenko standing in the farthest corner from the door, he knows Chenko has had his eyes fixed on him from the moment he opened the door. Linwood begins, "Saw your truck - tried all the doors. The Lord led me to this one and opened it for me," to cover himself. Chenko wants to roll his eyes, but forces a smile. "Yeah, hear there isn't a door he can't open," Linwood answers, "Amen."

Seems the Lord is always with Linwood, and as the deal on the dresser goes forward it's more that Linwood tells the Lord what to do, than the other way around. Linwood hands Chenko a new card. Again, it's as if he's won another award. Only this time Chenko becomes more aware during the presentation that Linwood has spent a lot time in front of the tube. He's locked on to all the stations run by televangelists. His appearance makes him look like one, especially the attention grabbing suit and the way he wears his hair, slicked back, always giving the impression he knows what he's talking about.

He pays little attention to the theology Linwood tries to convey after the deal, for the most part Chenko responds with polite nods to Linwood's view of how the Lord brought them together, a view Chenko doesn't share. After the theatrical evangelizing of something deeper than a business deal, Linwood expects a lot of questions. But the only questions Chenko asks are "This is your number, cell or home? This address is your current location?" Linwood answers both. "Cell" and "yes" and gives a puzzled look as if Chenko has missed something really important.

But Linwood likes what he sees and the two work a deal, he'll take the dresser and Chenko will get a $125, Linwood $50, if it moves during the winter. Chenko is okay with the deal, other than its purchase price, he didn't have to put any money into it and if it doesn't move, at the end of winter Chenko gets it back. To Chenko it's a subconscious down payment on getting through the winter, his deal with the devil. Linwood will call once a month with an update. For a moment Chenko begins to calculate the time in dog years, but abandons the calculation to help Linwood put the dresser on the trailer.

He does ask Linwood about the car. "How'd you come by the Pacer?" Chenko is now in the mood for some conversation, but Linwood is not and answers with a curt "The Lord." Chenko smiles, his reply bordering on sarcasm... "Should've known." Linwood nods and says nothing, he fires up the Pacer. The deal closes in what is becoming a terse and sarcastic atmosphere. Linwood's views rejected he becomes resentful. Chenko' refusal to understand will cost him. Linwood has a way to punish him.

The dresser is off the floor. Chenko thinks Linwood has just the dresser, but he has more. During the negotiations, Chenko, out of cigars, goes to Old Red to get some, leaving Linwood alone in the office. On his desk, in a stack of papers that should be in a drawer, is an old license registration with a lot of personal information, ownership and insurance for one, his Social Security number and home address for another. The registration isn't in view, but not hard to find. Linwood feels led by a higher authority to put some of this information in his cell phone. In the future he and the Lord will create a new Ananias Zachenko.

Chenko shakes his head a few times as he walks back to the fire, hearing, but not seeing Linwood leave. As the crunching sound of gravel ceases, he pulls a chair in front of the stove and thinks more of Linwood than the deal. He lights a cigar and exhales. "Who was that masked man?"

On one hand, Linwood has the ability to be fluid in what he says, on the other; what he says is far from clear. He's as out of touch as the suit he's wearing. The framework of his mind is built by the tele-evangelists. During the dresser deal Chenko learned how Linwood has been anointed, tithes, the religious gifts he has from his love offerings, how the end is at hand, how godless we've become and the seeds he's planted.

But what concerns Chenko the most is they never shook hands on the deal and for some reason not doing so seems more natural. And Chenko gives himself credit for knowing the atmosphere wasn't right for that to take place.

A plume of cigar smoke finds Chenko's eyes. Chenko blinks his burning eyes a few times and tries to focus on the new card Linwood gave him. He goes to his desk and searches for the old card Linwood gave him, wondering if both were the same. The card he used for the call was on the center of the desk, when he gets to the desk he can't find it anywhere on the surface. It isn't until he looks at the floor that he finds the card. For a moment he wonders how it got there, but then picks it up and starts to compare the two. Nothing is the same. He sees in the past two or three years Linwood has changed locations and makes a mental note. "I have two locations." Chenko then wonders, "How'd the call get through? He's got more than one number too." It was strange but not a mystery. Chenko staples the cards together and puts them in the false bottom box, muttering to himself "Want to keep both eyes on this boy."

He returns to the stove and stokes the fire more to watch the flames than do anything constructive. A small wooden barrel is by the chair in front of the stove. He gets a beer from the refrigerator, sets some cigars on the barrel along with his lighter and cell phone, then the beer, and decides to have another shot of Dickel before sitting down. He drags an over-stuffed chair, known as the "Uncle Bart" next to the stove. It showed up one day a long time ago for repair and it never left, its constant use by the inner circle preventing its repair. His plan is to drink the beer and take a "chair" nap.

The nap is interrupted by a background of flames and the conscious vision of sitting in one of the many classrooms in University Hall at Ohio State. In this building Chenko completed his Humanities requirements and God did come up as a topic for discussion through Friedrich Nietzsche, Thomas Paine, Thomas Jefferson, Karl Marx and a host of others. They provide the other side of the story to Chenko's adolescent church upbringing. The flames hypnotize Chenko; he goes to a time and place when unisex long hair, flannel shirts, sandals, field jackets, P coats and jeans of the late '60s were the fashion for twenty-year olds.

The time and place in the past provided the background to his mental wrestling match about the existence of God. Ever since his diagnosis God keeps popping up in his thoughts on a more regular basis. He becomes lost in memories, and if Linwood's visit had any purpose, it probably would be found in returning to this building and topic. To a time and place where he'd walk into a room with one set of beliefs and came out an hour later with another set.

He sits comfortably and has the time to review all the impact statements he's heard on God. The first one, Friedrich Nietzsche proclamation: "God is dead." Some long forgotten ill-dressed professor in the Hall answers its resurgence during the time with "The human concept of God makes this impossible. God and death are mutually exclusive. God is the exclusion of death and death is the exclusion of God."

Chenko buys into the reasoning. Chenko believes the rule of exclusion to be true, he was brought up with the scriptures and the exclusion of God as the form death takes is mentioned more than once, the idea God is dead never held any weight with him. The ill-dressed professor's eloquent presentation reinforces his belief that Nietzsche's assertion is false.

Then there's the question "Did God create man or did man create God?" Chenko can't remember who asked it, but in one of the classrooms he remembers he agreed with the answer given in the lecture on the question by the same professor. It comes down to the 'wants and needs' of God and man. These two words can create a series of 'If and Then' statements to help answer the question. Whenever the word 'create' is used substitute either word or combination of the two. For example, "If God wants man, then man needs God. If God needs man, then man wants God," and so on, the entire set of 'If and Then' statements leading to an answer that what exist are the wants and needs of both God and man; the original question of creation secondary to the existence of want and need in the relationship.

We know we exist; the question is does God? But it would seem if God doesn't exist then we wouldn't have a term for such a being. The question is really more a statement of existence through want and need, than a question of who created who. Some believe the first part (God created man), others the second part (man created God), the two beliefs always in conflict with each other. All we know is one part is right and the other wrong, but which? The question can't be answered now. But in the end, all will know. For now, the question is the mystery of faith.

There's a pile of split wood by the stove and Chenko grabs two pieces and stokes the fire, he doesn't want to lose the flames. When they reach the right level, he settles back into the Uncle Bart and picks up where he left off. He puts his beer down and concludes he did all right in the Humanities, they were 'cume' builders, and given the passage of time, he's somewhat impressed and surprised with himself that he can recall more than a few lectures. He knows he wasn't shy about blowing off class if it interfered with his non-classroom education. He definitely completed more hours in non-classroom studies. His grades reflected this; he was no stranger to bar rooms and bedrooms.

But of all the lectures heard and argued in both classroom and barroom no one could doubt the logic behind *Pascal's Wager,* although some tried. Simply put – *By believing in God one has everything to gain and nothing to lose. By not believing in God, one has everything to lose and nothing to gain* – which way would you wager? And 'wager' here would be another word for 'hope.'

The thought takes Chenko to the equation he formed from the start to get more time, 'hope' being a major factor in its calculation. The scriptures are built on hope and for a moment he tries to recall one, but can't. Not one he can directly quote, but he knows there's a part in the scriptures where God instructs Moses to tell Pharaoh "I AM." It's enough to hedge his bet on the first part of the wager.

It was good for Chenko to gather in his personal theology against a background of flames. It was something needed and long overdue given his condition. He never had a problem with the Father, Son and Holy Ghost, he's called on all three at different times in certain situations, but he's also taken their name in vain at different times in certain situations. He's always been pro and con on the Trinity. As far as the scriptures go, he questions some, but agrees with most. Chenko believes God gives him the right to question and the choice to believe. It's a simple theology, childlike.

He takes another pull from his beer and lights another cigar, now starting to chain smoke, then he moves the chair back from the heat of the fire. He's amazed at how deep his thoughts are. He thinks of The God of Abraham and scriptures from the Torah, Bible and Koran, the three books written about this God and the shared prophets. All are the same and yet different. All subject to interpretation that has brought forth both good and evil. The good comes from God's knowledge; the evil comes from man's formation of religion to deal with this knowledge. The fact is, these different interpretations or religions, of the same God, often cause conflict,not agreement. Religious wars fill a big part of history. Religion is a paradox to Chenko.

For a moment he sees the earlier part of the afternoon and Linwood standing by the fire. Linwood attempting some moral high ground about how God is no longer a part of the government, schools, our institutions, and laments as a society we've abandoned God. Now Chenko wishes he would have answered Linwood with more than nods and chides himself. What Linwood was really saying is 'his religion' is no longer a part of these institutions. Now if Linwood was there, right now, he'd let him know how he felt about this position "God was never meant to be part of these institutions, God left that up to us through the gift of logic and reason, end of subject, subject closed."

But if Linwood would've wanted to continue, Chenko is now more than willing to give his view and he carries on his imaginary rebuttal. "Look at it this way Linwood, to follow the doctrines and dogmas of religion in blind faith has always led to trouble. Blind faith creates more problems than it solves. History is full of the difficulties this blindness has caused. When it comes to faith I want full vision. I agree with Thomas Paine: "*My mind is my own church.*"

The Founding Fathers got it right in Article VI, Clause III: *No religious test shall ever be required as a qualification to any office or public trust of the United States."* (Chenko remembers this because he missed article and clause on a test in college; getting these two right, which he didn't at the time, the difference between a C and a D. He's remembered the passage ever since). This Article and Clause only mentions religion, not God. C'mon Linwood uses your head; can you imagine how crazy it'd be if religion was a test? God let us write it this way, God's still around."

If Linwood didn't buy into this Chenko was ready to take it to the next level. "C'mon Linwood...get your head out of your ass. These self-righteous carnies on TV are playing you with their revelations, anointments, offerings, gifts, seeds, and blessings. All have a price tag, all for sale at the bottom of screen, all can only be purchased with a "love offering, call the number today, have your credit card ready.

They're selling you a pretty simple diet – keep sending money and everything will be okay - when it isn't - it's because you don't believe enough - send more. The people who buy into them are the same people who believe Big Time Wrestling is real. They're a side show. These guys cherry pick the Bible, Jefferson did too, but he didn't try to sell it. They make Karl Marx look like he was right *"Religion is the opiate of the masses."* They're not praying for you – they're preying on you. So there. Put this in your pipe and smoke it."

Chenko lets the flames die down after releasing his venom. He sits in an atmosphere of anxiety. Thinking of Linwood makes his lower back start to ache. He gathers his belongings from the barrel and begins to wonder why God would put Linwood in his path at that this point in the game. For a few moments he looks for some hidden purpose. He has no idea how much time he'll gain by trying to keep his eyes on this boy. As he leaves, he's struck by a strange thought, the second meeting didn't end like the first, there is no "Be seeing you" and this bothers him. A cloud of cigar smoke covers his words as he locks the door. "This is more than a $100 deal."

******

The atmosphere isn't getting any better. A low-grade fever has become the sidekick of the lower back pain. "Why is this happening?" There's no need to ask the question, Chenko knows why. Chenko treats the fever as an inconvenience. He sits at home in front of the computer on his desk electronically going over his accounts. He wants to remain current on their activity, but is overwhelmed by his condition.

It's nothing he can't work through, but knows what afflicts him will soon no longer be a secret if he doesn't see a doctor. Ilene wasn't smiling the other night like she was about a month ago, when she mentioned his weight. The smile is starting to change to a look of concern. The activity he's looking at will eventually double in size, but not all will be due to his decision to reenter treatment. A second front in his war for survival is about to open up.

The back and now the fever make him more aware some people are going to have to know. Otherwise at the rate he's going they'll figure it out and all he'll get from them is their pity. He rather let them know what he faces upfront and then let them judge how well he handles it. He wants to be remembered as one who dictated the terms of his death, going farther with his condition than anyone expected on the way to his seventh star.

He returns to the rocket he wants to launch, the second phase of what needs to be accomplished before the third phase, the heroic act he has planned for when he runs out of dog years. He vows by sunset tomorrow his family will know. He grabs a handful of paper from the printer tray by the computer, sticks a pen in his pocket, moves his glasses to the top of his head, shuts down the computer and heads to the barn where he can smoke. Before the end of tomorrow all his thoughts will be put to paper and he'll know what to say and say it.

The control for the garage door opener attached to the wall doesn't work. Another headache; Ilene has mentioned the problem more than once. What works are the remotes in her car, Chenko's truck and the outside keypad. It would seem to be enough, but within the last few days, the garage door has developed a mind of its own, sometimes it stays down, other times it goes down and then right back up. To get it to stay down you have to waste time playing the remote or keypad. It drives Ilene nuts. If he didn't have important thoughts to put down, Chenko would first try to fix the situation and then second, have someone come out. He wants to fix the door, but needs to gather his thoughts before tomorrow's sunset. The garage door is just part of the atmosphere he's trying to survive.

Chenko squeezes between the rear bumper and garage door, walking like a pair of scissors, wrestles past the shelves, hanging bikes, sleds and stationary equipment to the driver's side of Old Red. He gets in, sits behind the wheel turns the key and through a cloud of cigar smoke sees the orange extension cord in front of the satchel on the third shelf in the corner of the garage. He locks on to the cord, not the satchel, and thinks "Good," the cord won't be a mystery when he has to string the Christmas lights. Presses the remote on his visor and waits for the garage door to go up, thinking the atmosphere will improve after this mission to the barn, then the garage door will get fixed and the lights will go up. Everything will be different.

As the garage door slowly makes its way up the rails, Chenko's rearview mirror is filled with the unexpected, the front end of a 1963 black Cadillac Coup-Deville in near mint condition. There's a guy standing by the drivers' side door. The guy is making no attempt to move and has him boxed in.

Chenko gets out and wrestles his way to the open garage door wondering who this guy is. It isn't until he is face to face that he recognizes Seth Brandsome (Brandsome the

Handsome) a guy Chenko drank with for about a year and a half after he got out of the Army and before he got married. The first year and half he worked at the rubber shop and had some money. Seth has changed.

"Chesterfield told me where to find you," Seth begins. Chenko is at loss for words; he just shakes his head, and in a rare gesture gives Seth a short hug to make up for the time it took to recognize him. "Yeah. I know," Seth says in return to the gesture and adds "I'm now 'Seth the wreck.'" Chenko thinks, but doesn't show he's right, the thick full dark hair is down to a few strands, Seth's unlined chiseled face now full of lines and cracks, his glowing complexion is grey and his perfect physique withered.

It doesn't matter; Chenko still pictures him in his early twenties as Brandsome the Handsome. "Relax - we all got a little road rust," he tells Seth, smiling. "Chesterfield was supposed to send me some tickets. Let's get something to drink. What ya drinking?" It's an attempt to make it seem like old times. Seth slightly tilts his head to the left, like always, smiles and answers... "Milkshakes."

Chenko's unconscious gesture and Seth's answer, along with his appearance, tells Chenko, Seth is a "dead man walking." There's now a mirror in front of Chenko instead of Seth. "Let's get one," Chenko tells him, unable to camouflage his concern, what's in front of him now more important than the mission he's on. He becomes aware this is a glimpse into the future. The fact that no alcohol is mentioned is ignored, where once it would've been questioned. "Let's go," he answers Seth

"Slide on in, my man," Seth invites. In a matter of seconds, as he walks to the passenger door, Chenko recalls all he can about Seth. He's struck by all that passes through his mind in such a short walk, opens the door and gets in. The impact of the brief period they spent together still felt. In the space of time it takes him to get in, a year and half of total nonsense flashes across his mind like a rocket that eventually disappears into the atmosphere.

Last thing Chenko heard about Seth is that he won the lottery and that was more than thirty years ago, the popular reason he dropped off everyone's radar. Seems Seth was always around and then one day gone with no warning, nothing said, just gone.

But when he was around, he became someone one wouldn't forget. He had the gift of gab and the women loved him. He had graduated from college, been in the war, had a great job and never missed a day of work. These attributes were coupled with an incredible tolerance for alcohol and drugs and a huge appetite for life in the fast lane. Back then he was the total package.

Seth knew all the dancers at the Back Bar and introduced Chenko to every one of them. In the beginning it was nice, but Chenko tired of hearing about their boyfriends in prison and the guns and cocaine that spilled from their purses during the one-night stands. Every one of them was a victim of their own beauty.

It was a period of flesh and no spirit. Seth has no problem leaving with a dancer every time they're at the bar. But when Chenko eventually gets his turn with each and asks about their nights with Seth all admit they never slept with Seth and it wasn't that they didn't want to. Chenko doesn't know what to believe, on one hand, Seth tells a different story, on the other, it could be one of the few experiences the dancers want to keep private, but after a while what he is told, from more than one, makes him wonder. Maybe it wasn't the lottery, but something else that made him disappear, doesn't matter now.

As they begin to pull out Chenko casually tells Seth, "Hold up. Gotta get the door." He gets out and plays the outside keypad and on the fourth try gets the door to stay down. "Got the dancing door, huh, Chenko?" Chenko shakes his head. "I got the Fred Astaire." Seth laughs and tells Chenko "You look good man." For a moment Chenko thinks, compared to what - you? He doesn't say this, but instead tells Seth, "I'll tell you what looks good is this ride" and runs his hands over the dashboard and radio. "So, where the hell you been?"

Chenko directs Seth to Betty's and they begin to make up for lost time. Seth answers Chenko's questions on how he came by the Sixty-three Caddy and they recall Jimmy Chesterfield's cage fighter. As they head down the road the small talk ends and Chenko hears of Seth's brothers and sisters, they never came up once when they ran together. Seth has been introduced to Chenko's brothers at one time or another, and heard of his sister, but this is the first time Chenko learns Seth has brothers and sisters, four of each!

Somehow it didn't seem natural. Seth was always one of a kind; one couldn't see him sharing the stage with anyone, even brothers and sisters. But he tells Chenko he'd just recently seen all of them, listed their names and that was about all. Next Chenko learns that Seth was on the ground floor of Silicon Valley when it took off and made a ton of money early, too early. He never married, had any kids, and never lived longer than two years anywhere, been north, south, east and west over and over again. Once he left a place he never kept in touch.

They make their way across the parking lot. Once inside Chenko guides Seth to his corner booth. Audrey comes over and starts. "Twice in one day? Really?" Chenko pays no attention to the remark and orders. "We're here for the endless shake, I'd like the first half of my chocolate shake mixed thin, the second half mixed thick and then poured in a large soup bowl, bring me two straws and a soup spoon with it." Audrey tries not to laugh, nods. "Right." She looks at Seth sympathetically knowing whose company he's in, hoping for a normal response, but Seth answers with a smile. "The same." She tells Seth, "You're not right either, are ya?" before walking to the soda fountain.

"She's easy on the eyes," Seth comments. "You know all the girls in here, don't you?" Chenko nods and is struck by the reversal of fortune, there was a time when he was the one asking that question.

Seth leans forward putting both arms on the table and slides the salt shaker from hand to hand never taking his eyes off of it and begins to speak. "You know me, Chenko. I'll pull a cork or twist a cap on any bottle with anyone, toke and snort with them all night long too. Now, the shots and lines are different, so is the crowd, nothing but needles and bags, doctors and nurses." Chenko locks on to the salt shaker now and waits a few moments, all he can tell Seth is "You're in the dog years, man."

Seth looks up from the moving salt shaker at Chenko, who is still watching the shaker, and waits for Chenko to look up. Their eyes meet in total understanding and he tells Chenko... "Yeah, you're right. Dog years. I like it, sums it up".

Audrey brings the shakes as ordered, leaving them to their straws and soup spoons, both are a little surprised. Seth is impressed. Chenko then asks for crackers. Audrey tells Chenko "I'll bring you a mirror" As Seth watches her walk away, he tells Chenko "Been so many places, have to reintroduce myself to so many, just to say goodbye. Outside of my brothers and sisters, you're the first." Chenko is left speechless and is filled with the urge to tell Seth how he understands, that he's in his dog years too, but doesn't. He can't bring himself to do it.

Instead, he asks, "How long have you known?" Seth answers "It's been about three and a half very short years; everything is moving at the speed of light."

Chenko discovers that in the beginning Seth took the same approach Chenko is taking, about a half year ago he went back into treatment, but it's too late to buy time, now all treatment can buy is comfort.

The moment Chenko learns this, Seth becomes a benchmark, a mark that has to be surpassed. Three years seems a long way off especially the way Chenko feels. But Chenko sees the mistake Seth has made, he waited too long to go back into treatment. Chenko can no longer ignore the reflection in front of him. As much he hates the idea of reentry, Seth isn't giving him any options.

Chenko looks Seth in the eye and can no longer hold back the question he shouldn't ask, "AIDS?" Seth leans back from the table; he gives Chenko a forgiving laugh. "Know you've always thought that, but no, it's cancer." For a moment Chenko wants to defend himself by telling Seth he's talked to the dancers. But there's no suitable explanation for the question. Seth knows what he's asking. The thought leaves as quickly as it came. He tells Seth... "Doesn't matter. Everyone gets a death sentence. I got one coming and yours is here, that's the way it works. There's no pill for the pain of knowing." Seth teases Chenko with a question "Dog years start when you find out?" But it really isn't a question; it's his way of letting Chenko see he might know more than Chenko thinks. Chenko can only nod, unable to speak.

The afternoon odyssey ends as it began with Seth's Sixty-three Caddy in Chenko's driveway. They're back to small talk and a few old memories, nodding and laughing. Chenko gets out and gives Seth a final nod. Seth leans towards the driver's door and tells Chenko "Turns out, I know everybody from everywhere, but don't know one soul from one place." These are his last words to Chenko; he then backs down the driveway and disappears for good.

******

The situation with the garage door can no longer be ignored. Chenko has it in writing on the kitchen counter. The note is pretty direct. Since his visit with Seth more than one sunset has passed with nothing said to his family. It's taken a little time to shake off Seth. He's hasn't been able to complete his mission or fix the door, but at the same time is as close to completing both as he's ever been. His pent-up emotions are about to be released.

If Ilene had not left the number for the guy, mentioning he fixed the door about five years ago, Chenko would be releasing these emotions at the barn.

One thing about Ilene, she's the most organized person Chenko knows. Another, she's tolerant to a point, a point one doesn't want to reach. Chenko knows he's very close to that point. In fairness to Ilene, the door problem has been going on for over a week. She's barely over five feet and doesn't weigh any more than one hundred eight pounds, but she can become twice her size if she has to. She works hard all day and doesn't need to wrestle a garage door when she gets home. Chenko understands this, and feels bad it's come down to a note and wishes she really knew why it's taken so long.

He can picture her: dark hair slightly shaking, brown eyes flashing, she's standing as she writes the note, one foot on the floor, the other slightly raised, all the colors she's wearing match and accent her nice figure. He knows exactly how the notes are written, he's seen her do it before, seen her write the good and the bad; he doesn't need to use his imagination. It's like she's standing there when he reads it. He's still attracted to her. The door will be fixed before she gets home, followed by an apology.

Chenko looks at the number and wonders if the guy is still in business (CDA - Garage Door). Next, he wonders the odds, if he gets an answer, of getting on the schedule for the day. For a moment the odds he's giving himself makes him think of Linwood. But Linwood comes and goes as Chenko begins to conjure up a huge garage door emergency, one no person with a conscience could ignore, before dialing the number.

On the second ring Chenko gets an answer. He begins to describe his calamity, the guy on the other end interrupting him for an address. Chenko stops in his tracks at the part about how they were unable to get a hospital bed in the house for an invalid family member and gives it to him. The guy reads it back and responds with "Be there in thirty minutes." Chenko replies "Great!" He hangs up and goes to the garage and moves Old Red to the street and starts to straighten up the place.

He begins a thorough sweeping campaign, rearranging some things, and starts at the farthest corner of the garage. As he concentrates on his sweeping, he takes a moment to move the extension cord from the shelf to Ilene's side of the garage, puts it on her potting table so it will be in full view.

He fills the open space on the shelf with some paint cans; next he places a folded step ladder in front of the cans and continues sweeping. He's unaware his actions put the missing satchel completely out of view. During the cleanup he thinks of his re-entry into treatment and how he needs to find the satchel.

Exactly thirty minutes after the phone call, a faded tan cargo van pulls in the drive way. On its sides CDA – Garage Door, a short stocky guy, who's seen more than one diner, gets out, takes off his ball cap and looks at the garage. Chenko is standing at the center of the garage and waits to be noticed. "Did a spring here once, 'bout five years back," the guy says. Chenko nods, and thinks Ilene mentioned this in her note and replies "I know," as if he's always known, then the guy introduces himself, "I'm Voegie."

The two begin to talk; Chenko takes out his cigars and offers one to Voegie. "I shouldn't, damn things will kill ya." But willingly takes a light from Chenko. By the time they finish their smokes Chenko learns in twenty minutes that Voegie has installed and fixed all types of garage doors for more than twenty-five years. That CDA stands for Canton Detective Agency and that when his dad quit being a detective and moved into garage doors, he just kept the CDA and added "garage door" - cheaper. It's an interesting story how Voegie got into the business. Chenko also learns Voegie is blue collar, after the smoke break, he wants to get to work.

"So, what's the problem?" Voegie asks and Chenko demonstrates with the remote and outside key pad, as the door goes up and down, like jump rope, he and Voegie time their way to the pad inside the garage, Chenko presses it to demonstrate it doesn't work as the garage door continues to go up and down. With the remote Chenko finally gets the door to stop in the up position.

Voegie asks "Where's your breaker?" The two wander to the circuit breaker box in the basement; look at the mapping on its metal door, which has been modified more than once, and then the alignment of the breaker switches.

Within a few seconds they find a thrown switch, but the garage door isn't mapped to the switch, doesn't matter it's switched back to "On." They return upstairs; Chenko presses the pad by the door and the garage door starts its dance. Voegie just looks at Chenko, the solution so simple; there is no need to mention how simple. His posturing lets Chenko know Voegie isn't the dumbest guy in the garage. The attitude doesn't bother Chenko, after this little exercise he knows it's well deserved.

In Chenko's defense what was mapped to the switch are some seldom used outlets and closet lights in the laundry room. Their lack of use the reason he never thinks of the breaker box. Chenko knows at best this would be a thin excuse and decides to say nothing and move with Voegie to the next problem, the dancing door.

Voegie watches it go up and down several times, studying its every move. He takes the remote from Chenko and on the first try stops the door half way down. Then he goes to the right end of the door and looks down the galvanized metal strip at the bottom of the door, like one looks down a rifle barrel. He goes to the left end and repeats the process.

Next, he steps back and centers himself on the door and looks at the strip and both ends again. Voegie takes off his cap, runs one hand over the top of his head then puts it back on. Walks to one end then the other, runs his hands over each end and then shows Chenko a half hand full of what he calls "door lint," the wispy fibers that once made up the leaf that got stuck between the metal strip and bottom of the door.

The fibers are hardly noticeable in his hand, but enough to interfere with the signal from one electric eye to the other. The eyes are clipped to the bottom of the garage door rails. They're enough to break the signal to go down; when it's broken the door goes up. Because it didn't go down all the way, when it goes up, it goes up farther than it should and triggers a signal to go down. "Door lint... It's something you don't think about," he tells Chenko.

Voegie drops the fibers on Chenko's clean floor. "Watch this." He goes to the pad by the door, presses it and the door goes down and stays down, presses it again it goes up and stays up. He does this five times and then Chenko does it five times. The solution was found in about five minutes. Voegie writes on his clipboard, taking on the mannerisms of a physician who has just healed a patient. He hands Chenko the bill, written on it... "TCB & EEI / DLR & DMO - $75." Chenko asks what it means, Voegie answers, "Thrown Circuit Breaker and Electric Eye Interference / Door Lint Removed and Door Made Operational, seventy-five dollars."

Chenko is silent for a few moments; he takes out his cigars and offers one to Voegie. Voegie views it as attempt to reduce the bill and refuses. Chenko realizes this and smiles. "Checkbook is in the truck." Voegie reacts. "On second thought, think I'll take that cigar.

The two begin to joke about the bill. Chenko starts... "Seventy-five Bucks! Hell! You didn't even get the tool box out!" Voegie laughs and replies, "Sometimes you're so good, you don't need it." He then gives Chenko a sly look and concludes... "Always good to know how to open and close a door."

As Chenko walks to Old Red he takes note of the time, thinking if he left for the barn in a half-hour, he'd get there earlier than usual. He reviews all that has happened, Voegie caught the phone on the second ring, showed up exactly when he said he would, wasn't hard to talk to, fixed everything in a minimum amount of time and educated him. Chenko writes the check for one hundred dollars.

When Voegie sees the check, he tries to refuse it, but like the second cigar, doesn't take long to finally accept it. He takes out his tool box and spends the next five minutes tightening all the nuts and bolts for the hinges and brackets on the garage door. The two thank each other, Chenko for the service, Voegie for the tip. Voegie gets in his van and drives off. He'll be back in about five years, Chenko thinks. He becomes another value in building the equation for more time. Chenko would like to see him again.

******

Chenko makes his way to the barn. He's following a Bucksworth Township maintenance truck driven by an old neighbor, Fred Dobson. Fred's in no hurry and all the time Chenko saved with Voegie is now being wasted by Fred.

But it might not be Freddy, could be the truck, it doesn't sound right, it's coughing some blue smoke. Chenko gives Freddy the benefit of the doubt that he's getting everything he can out of the truck; he always liked Fred, he knows Fred is just doing his job. He hopes Fred will turn down one of the many streets they pass, but Fred drives clear to the northeast end of the township past the barn and Chenko is the first to turn.

During the time-consuming ride, the weather and traffic makes passing Fred an unnecessary risk, Chenko doesn't want to think about his condition, but it's the only thought to surface in his attempt to take his mind off the aggravating truck in front of him.

At first, he's puzzled why he's feeling impatient and aggravated, but when he thinks of where he's going and why, he begins to understand. He can't find the words, but the search is on. As rare as the hug he gave Seth, he's at the point of tears. Like Fred's truck he's heading for a breakdown. Chenko forces them back and refuses to cry, it would've been better to let the tears go. It takes all his concentration to stop them. Concentration that would be better spent in coming up with what to say about his condition.

******

At the same time Chenko is holding back his tears, two townships away in a place called Barnwood, Linwood sits in a store front he's recently bought, the new home of The Never Ending True Vine Ministries. Linwood is filling out credit forms with the information he's gathered on three more non-believers he's recently come in contact with through his business that he will make anew.

He'll put them on a new path. He'll give them a mystery to solve. They will become part of his means to an end. Chenko is one of them. His desire is to build a ministry and find a station to carry his message. He's finally making his move to the "big time." This desire makes the means justify the end.

He's consumed with his mission. All he needs is a following and the support of those who already have a station. He wants to join their fraternity. He'll get their support with cash donated from his ministry to their causes until he and his ministry can't be ignored. They'll have to invite him on their shows and he'll move from there. Cash, especially from the three new people he's creating along with nine others, gives him a total of twelve, now has one for every month.

These are the last three Linwood needs, once a year Linwood will give them a mystery to solve. The twelve have no idea of their membership in NETV Ministries. Chenko's month is coming in the near future.

The storefront has a large professionally done sign that adds some legitimacy. The sign overlooks a fair size parking lot. The sign paid for by one of his members who is about to receive their first mystery. The inside has been remodeled; there are enough pews to hold five hundred people. The church hasn't officially opened, but he has Photo shopped flyers he's about to send out in which both the pews and parking lot are packed. There's a new men's and woman's restroom for the phantom congregation.

There is a large professionally done solid oak altar centered on a stage. It is in front of a curved high quality large purple curtain that runs ceiling to floor on the stage. Above a chair, that is painted gold resembling a throne, and centered on the curtain, is his logo. It's well-done in sheet metal and resembles a large gold coin about eight feet in diameter. It hangs from two barely visible wires giving it the appearance of floating in air. The coin depicts a dove descending on the head of a man wearing a garland of grape vines; the top edge of the large coin reads "NETV Ministries," the bottom edge "The One and Only Way Home."

Behind the curtain are four rooms. A meditation room that borders on the edge of being a good place for a lap dance. It leads to an office, with a private bathroom that has all the amenities. The bathroom has two doors. The door from the office at one end and another door at the other end leading to a spacious bedroom with huge mirrors and closets. All the rooms are furnished with the high-end antiques of the business Linwood is no longer in; Chenko's dresser is in the far corner of his bedroom.

It would be Chenko's luck to run into Linwood's side show at this stage of his life. What kind of luck still to be determined. As he sits in his office, paper on the desk, pen in hand, looking out the window. Chenko unaware, along with eleven others, of what is taking place two townships away lights a cigar and finally begins to write.

"Been to the doctors, they tell me I have a year left.

I don't believe them.

I believe in you, Eve and Hope.

So far, it's been a good journey.

We'll keep on the path.

Promise …

I didn't spend forty years in the wilderness with you…

You've always been my promised land…

I don't see an end in sight."

Chenko puts the pen down and reads what he has written. As he reads in cloud of cigar smoke the events of the past few weeks flash through his mind. He sees Linwood, Seth and Voegie: Linwood the evangelist, Seth "the mirror" and Voegie the physician. They all showed up for a reason, but at this point what holds Chenko's interest is what he has just put to paper. They weren't the best words, but there'd be no rewrite. They're enough. From this point on there is no turning back. He spends the rest of the afternoon memorizing these sixty words. Chenko can repeat them forwards and backwards. They will be the only words he'll know until sunset. By the time the sun sets on the two townships that day, in less than sixty seconds, Ilene knows and the atmosphere changes.

CHAPTER IV:
CONSTELLATIONS

T he constellations are the first maps, clocks, and keys to travel from one stage to another in unlocking the future," Chenko thinks to himself. For the past few days, they've been on his mind. He's taken to reading his horoscope in the paper on regular basis.

To take his mind off the constellations he stands by the fire and looks at the huge vanity with its large mirror he's just moved from Goodwill to his barn. He's been in the false bottom box. He's also made a few trips to the ice box to see his friend George Dickel and together they've built the nice fire he's standing next to. The snow-covered fields and woods fill the view from the windows and on his desk in the office there's a fresh box of cigars waiting for him.

The dresser is a unique piece, two six drawer pedestals, a middle drawer, solid wood top. A feminine piece designed to hold cosmetics and lingerie; it has a three foot by four-foot mirror attached to reflect the results of their application and choice of apparel. It's designed for a house that has a lot of square footage. At one time it cost a lot. It's probably a solid maple piece, but hard to tell, it's seen more than one finish. The lines of the piece show the simplistic look of the late Fifties or early Sixties, they're clean and Chenko plans to find its natural finish.

He'll strip it, sand it, rub it out with a linseed oil and beeswax paste, swap out the hardware. The hardware will require some thought. The right hardware will move the piece. He visualizes the type he wants. He wants something as simple as the piece. Something maybe he could make. The vanity offers all the challenges he wants, it will take some time to do it right. He smiles. It will take him deep into winter, only one more piece of hardware has to be finished and put on. He never gets to it.

Chenko is in a good mood. Christmas has come and gone and given the sixty word bomb he dropped on Ilene and the kids there's been an adjustment that, so far, isn't as severe as expected. All survived the shock wave, but that's not to say they aren't shaken.

Now that it's out in the open with the immediate family, Chenko wouldn't be Chenko if he didn't try to take advantage of the new situation created by his confession. This is the way he lets Ilene, Eve and Hope know he's still the same. He gives them what they expect.

After a night or two of tears and explaining the dog years and the seventh star to them and that Lefty, Flossie, Morton and Al have known from day one, which in a strange way his audience kind of understand, Eve and Hope break the ice. Eve asks "Does this mean you can't help build my deck this spring?"

Hope adds "What about the painting you were going to do for me?"

Chenko answers both with a long smile. "Whoa! Talk about something up in the air! ...I don't know. I'm pretty sick, I don't know if Mr. Tomb will allow that."

Their approach and his like two cold fronts running into each other and for some unknown reason begin to change into a warm front.

He makes his wife and children aware he's made his disease a person he has no respect for, always mocking what this person will do next. Neither the husband or father they know is afraid of this person and if he is, he isn't going to show it. He doesn't fear the person, but he does fear the disease the person carries.

It's simple: to get rid of the disease get rid of the person. Chenko names the person "Mr. Tomb." Mr. Tomb is responsible for the condition he's in, and Ilene, Eve and Hope, begin to hear all the plans Chenko has to kill him. He lets them know he has no conscience when it comes to Mr. Tomb, first chance he gets and without batting an eye he's going down. What he tells them in general is reassuring, what he tells them about his plans for Mr. Tomb is frightening.

The only down side, so far, is now there are three women involved in the situation. There is total involvement by all three in scheduling of appointments, keeping appointments, and the complete debriefings after these appointments. Chenko knows from here on out it is far better to know when the appointment is, keep it and report back, than to do otherwise. Their total involvement has given him total awareness. It would be better to have not been born than cross anyone of them. Conversations now always revolve around whom he's seen, what was done and what they said. He's hemmed himself in.

Chenko lights a cigar and pulls Uncle Bart closer to the fire. His work for the day is over, getting the vanity to the barn. In the past two weeks he's put on five pounds and doesn't have any new aches and pains. He feels better.

There's no smoking at home anymore, and he believes the way everything is going there's really no need for reentry. Doesn't matter, after the sixty words bomb the appointments will be made and soon, he'll be keeping them. He'll try to do what the doctors tell him, but will reserve some rights; he's more committed than ever, and his wife and children get him moving in the direction the doctors couldn't. Playing ball with the medical and insurance industries again is the price he has to pay, but they're not going to own him.

As he sits in front of the fire his thoughts move from reentry, to hardware design, to the 'cold case' file of his mind, he asks himself, "What happened to the satchel?" He goes over and over in his mind the day it disappeared, but nothing surfaces. All that surfaces is his need. He gets a beer and sits back down and ignores the reentry, hardware and satchel to return to the first thought of the day, the constellations.

Seems he dreamed of a new one the night before or maybe a week ago. He can't decide when, but since that night the dream comes and goes at will, it's back and is what holds his attention as he settles comfortably into Uncle Bart.

The influence of the false bottom box, George Dickel and the Coors family are starting to kick in. Chenko knows it'll be a while before he'll get another opportunity to spend an afternoon like this. He decides to spend the whole afternoon in their company and expand his mind. He'll go anyplace his company wants to go and, on the way, make up for all the smoking he's missed at home. Soon, the way he's spending this afternoon, he'll be told is the absolute last thing he should be doing. There will be plenty of doctors and family to remind him of this.

His wife and children will always be able to catch the slight scent of tobacco and alcohol, but the scent will become weaker. Chenko's progress with them will be based on the strength of his scent. When it becomes too strong Ilene, Eve and Hope will more than let him know, subconsciously this is how the game will be played. There will be no back sliding. But for the time being this afternoon is not an opportunity to pass up.

Chenko sits with his company and marvels at the flames in the primeval comfort man has always known from the moment man had time to enjoy the visual warmth it provides. The fire is the earliest form of entertainment, ancient TV. It's human nature not to pass up the opportunity to sit by a fire. He tunes into the time Travel Channel of his mind as the flames hold his gaze, not into the future, but into the past.

Again, the dream reminds him. He sees himself as a man from an ancient time, perhaps the end of the Stone Age. When obsidian and flint have been developed as far as possible and the transition to metal at hand, a Neolithic man at the point of this transition of good stature, dressed comfortably in cloth and fur. Both stature and dress provided by the development of stones and ore. He sees himself on a warm spring night on the side of a grassy hill comfortably looking into the heavens.

His company urges him on. This is what Chenko tells them. It's all brought on by the dream. The dream he is beginning to research. He's never had any interest in the constellations, but since the dream has read up on them. He learns their names are in Latin and from Andromeda to Vulpecula there are eighty-eight internationally known constellations. There are northern and southern constellations, and he becomes aware there are only twelve that most people pay attention to, the twelve signs that make up the Zodiac and their horoscope.

The Zodiac some say has its origins in Babylon and showed up about a thousand years before Christ. If we take Christmas as His birthday, Christ is a Capricorn. The creatures of the Zodiac are in the Bible. The Zodiac has been around for a while and is common among several. The Chinese have their own in which the constellations are named after animals. He tells his company he remembers the year of the Rat.

He's read just enough on the Zodiac to be on the cusp of a dangerous fascination. As Chenko recalls in the dream, he's on the hillside looking at a clear star filled sky and discovers a seven-star constellation never known to the ancients, the Unknown Constellation of the Zodiac. It presents all kinds of problems. The potential for a Zodiac earthquake can't be overlooked. Now that it's been found, is it added to the Zodiac or does it replace a constellation?

The signs and horoscopes will change. There will be an army of astrologers taking one position or the other to deal with, people's signs will shift. People will become aware they're living the wrong temperament. No one would know the true answer to the often asked question, "What's your sign?" No one would know for sure. The discovery becomes a problem only he can solve.

Although he sees himself in an ancient time on the hill side, he has Twenty-first century knowledge. With that knowledge he'll be able to predict with great accuracy what is to come to the ancients. This advanced knowledge causes some anguish, should he set out from the hillside to let others know and change the Zodiac and their lives or does he keep the discovery to himself. This is the last conscious thought before the warmth of the fire, the Uncle Bart and the company he's been keeping put him to sleep and the second part of the dream unfolds.

A large gold coin floats in front of a purple background. The coin is larger than a wooden wagon wheel and Chenko can't make out what's on the face of the coin. He becomes so preoccupied with the coin and the purple-like sky it floats against that he doesn't notice the seven oracles who sit below the coin. They patiently wait to be noticed, arced behind an alter sitting on thrones, three on each side of the golden throne centered under the coin.

When he finally notices the oracles, Chenko recognizes every one of them. But he is unsure how he knows them. They're all familiar to him in a very uncomfortable way. He subconsciously begins to walk towards the Altar. The Altar is the only object between him, and the oracles and he stand before it and waits for someone to speak. A voice within him says "Always stay on this side of the Altar."

As Chenko waits he notices the similarities they share, all are dressed in fine expensive contemporary suits they've modified to reflect their individuality and importance. It's clothing he's seen before, yet different in a ridiculous way. They're not wearing the robes and hats of wizards one would expect. They've updated the appearance of such people. Each has his own monogram or symbol embroidered somewhere on their jackets, all wear expensive jewelry. They are Neolithic ancients dressed in contemporary clothing.

They introduce themselves as the Zealous Oracles (the ZO) and they are aware of Chenko's discovery. They refer to the Unknown Constellation as the "Hour Glass." The seven stars form an hour glass, this much they know, what they don't know is the part of heaven it occupies. What Chenko has found is not the Unknown Constellation, but the "Unknown Heaven." Six others have known the location of the Hour Glass, none are alive.

When Chenko hears this, an hour glass would make sense, although he sees it more as a "Z." It becomes clear to him he's the only living person who knows its location. It also becomes apparent that the six that preceded him didn't tell the ZO. There's the tradition. He decides to keep his discovery to himself. The ZO are not to know the location of the Hour Glass. They are not to find the Unknown Heaven. Heaven is to remain unknown to them.

As far as dreams go this dream would be no different in what does and doesn't make sense. Chenko, dressed in his cloth and fur, tells the "ZO" he's in his "Second Sputnik" of the universe. That he's engaged in a cold war and when this war ends, he'll then tell them what part of heaven the Hour Glass is in. For the time being his war takes precedent, he'll keep the intelligence to himself for tactical reasons.

He senses his appearance in comparison to the ZO, gives him an oracle, astrologer, or wizard status also, being perceived by the ZO as having powers he doesn't possess. The longer he talks the stronger this feeling becomes and he continues his bluff by telling them of three stage rockets and man-made stars whose distance from each other is measured in dog years. The ZO write it all down.

What he tells them is enough to hold the ZO's attention and he becomes as big a mystery to them as they are to him. They tell Chenko by their virtue he's still alive and with this virtue comes the obligation of letting them know the location of the Unknown Heaven. Chenko has been sent to them for a reason and they have been anointed as the ones to know so they can make this heaven known to all the congregations. But Chenko senses it's a self-anointment and no good could come of what they say. They want to control the horoscope of Hour Glass Constellation with their own theology, this is the way they will change the world. They're not to be trusted.

The part of the dream Chenko has that afternoon is a fitful conflict between him and the ZO. The ZO wants what he has and Chenko is unwilling to give it to them, sidestepping the issue with the war he has to win first. They would like to kill Chenko. But by virtue of what he knows they can't. As long as the ZO has no knowledge of the Unknown Heaven he will live for a while, he then wonders the ages of the six before him, feeling they were older than he is now when the ZO killed them. He knows from his dream when his time comes, he'll be the oldest. This is the only positive knowledge he has of the second part of his dream.

When Chenko awakes he is overcome by his dream. He sits in the Uncle Bart trying to make sense of it all as he watches the flames die while still held by their warmth. He goes over and over the dream while it is still fresh in his mind, but as the flames disappear and the area around the Uncle Bart grows cold, he's left with just one thought. The details of dream will fade with time, but the one thought he has is he has something someone wants. He can't give it to them if he wants to stay alive. The thought will always be with him.

He wrestles out of the hold the Uncle Bart has on him, taking a few seconds to get his balance, an effect brought on by the company he's kept and is a little unsteady as he stands by the stove. For a moment he chastises himself for the company he's kept, they mock him and seem unwilling to let him go. He rocks back and forth trying to find his center of gravity. He finds it and begins to slowly move. He shuts the vents on the stove and turns off the lights, finally making his way towards the door, he leaves his company blaming all of them for the second dream and tells them the dream means nothing to him, but this won't be the case.

The bright afternoon has turned dark and the wind is starting to pick up. Whatever warmth Chenko has from the fire is gone once he's outside. It's the first harsh weather of an Ohio winter that can make a short walk uncomfortable. The cab of Old Red it isn't any warmer, but there's no wind. He fires up Old Red and through a cloud of cigar smoke looks at the windshield hoping the wipers will remove the afternoon's snow. The wipers remove some of the snow, but the windshield must be scrapped. Chenko looks behind the passenger's seat for the scraper and some gloves. He finds the scraper, but no gloves. He swears under his breath, gets out and begins to scrape until his hands turn red and start to sting. The sting is starting to move up his arms, but before it hits the shoulders, he manages to scrape enough from the driver's side to give some limited visibility; the defroster will have to do the rest.

Chenko gets back in and holds his hands over the dashboard heat vents, just now starting to give some heat. He rubs them to regain the feeling he's lost. From the man-door to Old Red he's struck with a thought that shakes the very foundation of what he's been through, what he's going through and what he still has to go through. As he continues to rub his hands he begins to think, no one knows what they'll dream; a dream is something no one has control over. "What if I dream, I tell them? What if I don't stay on my side of the Altar?" he whispers to himself.

The dream about the Hour Glass constellation in the Unknown Heaven has been given in two parts and he knows somewhere along the line a third part will come, but when? It becomes a problem he will worry about from here on out. The third part will tell him more than he wants to know about the condition he is in. He'd never tell the ZO what they want while conscious, but what about when he's unconscious, like a dream he has no control over? As the heat builds up in the cab of Old Red so does his paranoia of the third part of his dream.

Chenko puts Old Red in gear and his foot on the brake, lost in thought. For a moment he wonders if he isn't starting to lose his mind. The engine is now running smooth and wants to move, but Chenko keeps his foot on the brake. He's still locked on his mind with all its dog years, Sputniks, cold wars, three stage rockets, seventh star, and satchel. The treatment he has to go through that seems to create all of them.

This along with cast of characters that have randomly crossed his path since he took up his unwanted mission, real and imagined and all that has happened since he was diagnosed. Chenko concludes that he isn't losing his mind, but he's close. He takes his foot off the brake and Old Red lunges into reverse for about five feet before Chenko can stomp on it again to gain control. The stop is abrupt. He then puts Old Red in Drive and gives it some gas and the snow crunches under the wheels as he slowly drives to the road that will take him home.

The windshield is clear and the cab is warm, but he's uncomfortable with the conclusions of the day as he rides home. It isn't real, yet it is, the day the ZO knows what he knows will be the day he dies. When the third part of his dream comes all will know. Chenko thinks all that crosses his mind from the afternoon is foolish, but at the same time knows what he has dreamt and that can't be changed. He'll always remind himself of the dream, both parts and the part to come. As he turns onto the last road home Chenko flicks his cigar from the window and exhales a cloud of yellowish smoke. "What an Afternoon."

******

In the weeks that follow the second part of his dream, Chenko begins a new routine centered on his treatment. He goes to his appointments, the barn, and then home. When he has no appointments he goes to Betty's then the barn, then home. He visits the Y every day now. Two days a week he swims. These are days one could see him twice at the Y. The other three days one would catch him just once, at the end of the day.

Now no matter the weekday between the barn and home he goes to the Y to shower and swap his scented clothes for the unscented he keeps in his locker. After a sauna and shower he works the toothpaste and deodorant in his shaving kit. He operates five days a week from one location to the other; the locations are like the stars in his own personal constellation that have to be visited to insure the future. He travels under his own sign and makes his own horoscope now.

The introduction of sauna, shower and change of clothes has cut into the time he spends with the company he's been known to keep and their afternoon visits are short. The effort to keep his family off his real scent has produced a sub-conscious moderation in bad behavior not due to a desire to change, but due to a lack of time.

Since its addition to his routine, Chenko has yet to fail a scent test; he makes sure he gives the aroma of a reformed person. His scent is still there, but it's a hint of what it really is, it's artificial, but if anything, the creation of the artificial scent isn't without its benefits in moderation and perception, it's not a total reformation, but a partial reformation.

Chenko has the doctors somewhat puzzled, but not totally. Scans have come back and although more than one organ is affected, there's been no movement in the terrorist cells, their invasion has stalled. The treatments have helped. The side effects of being extremely sensitive to the cold in touch and taste at times have produced the sting of an electrical shock with some voltage behind it. He has to force himself to eat and has had a few episodes passing what he's consumed. These side effects are not bad when compared to the nausea others get. Chenko always prefers pain over nausea. He feels fortunate these are the side effects he got.

There are few over the counter tablets from the health stores the doctors don't have a problem with, the majority of what he's taking have no effect. Some border on having a negative effect. The ones he's told are okay are okay more in a psychological sense, a placebo. The reduction in the volume of health store products is welcome relief from the pill popping he's been doing, not to mention the cost. He'll take the two the doctors say are okay only in the sense they are still part of his treatment for himself. The right mix of "his" and "their" treatment might be the answer. He'll try their way for a while now.

Chenko takes all their information and is willing to go with two tablets thinking if the terrorist cells start to move there will be another arms race in his cold war with them. If this happens, he's back to buying every anti-oxidant at the health store again. The boost from the health store is always there. This thought becomes Chenko's Plan B.

Seth Brandsome taught Chenko the importance of timing his re-entry. Seth waited too long. He lost his balance between tablet and treatment. He stayed in his own treatment past the point of no return. Chenko remembers how he told him he lasted three-and-a-half years this way, before buying time turned to buying comfort. When one starts buying comfort time begins to move at the speed of light. In less than sixty days Chenko will have completed seven dog years. In a little over two years, he'll tie Seth. The way Chenko is feeling, he doesn't see the tie as a problem.

Chenko is in remission. The doctors are upfront; they let him know nothing is going away. More than likely something will come along one day and set off the terrorist cells again and when it happens, they'll probably make up for lost time. They tell him it's still a "crap-shoot." Chenko thinks what in life isn't? For now, the scans are good, the space between treatments is growing, all he has to do is keep it this way.

The routine of traveling his constellation everyday helps in more than one way, the anxiety of the third part of his dream is also in remission. Plan A is to keep his condition and his dream in remission for at least forty-nine dog years. This will give him the time needed to reach the seventh star of what others call the Hour Glass constellation, the star that is the farthest distance from him in the Unknown Heaven.

After his "barn dream" there were a few nights of some wild dreams, but there is no relation to the Hour Glass and Unknown Heaven. There are snakes wearing vests playing a piano by slithering over the keys, the melody disturbing, but there are no oracles, no large coin, no purple background or thrones. For the most part there are good and bad dreams.

Most are good, in a short period of time sleep isn't a problem. This helps.

The immediate family knows his condition and this has reduced some of the pressure on Chenko, but increases it on Ilene, Eve and Hope. He's added some weight to their lives. His brothers and sister deserve to know. Each, in their way, has been good to him. It's been agreed Chenko will tell them, but for the time being he's feeling well enough to put this off for a while. For the time being those who have this knowledge will keep it to themselves, Chenko will know when the time is right to tell his brothers and sister. He loves them enough that he'll give them the minimum time to worry about him. His wife and children have told no one, but the pressure to talk to someone about him is starting to grow and occasionally, one will ask if he's told his family, hoping for a "yes" and getting a "no."

The routine increases his laundry. The locker at the Y is picking up his scent, to the point that the unscented he changes into are starting to smell like the locker. It's beginning to become counter-productive. Two nights back he could tell Ilene was right on the edge of saying something. Chenko solves the problem by getting a second locker. The old locker will hold the scented, the new the unscented. The new locker is on the other side of the locker room.

Chenko has his changing routine down pat, no one pays any attention or seems to notice him undressing in front of one locker and dressing in front of another. Both sides of the locker room know him. He secretly washes his clothes twice a week; for the most part the unscented get washed, Chenko always forgets the scented, sometimes the scented stay in the locker for more than a week and require a special wash.

Chenko puts three sets of scented clothes in the washer for a special wash, jeans, sweatshirts, socks and underwear. Puts it on a "hot/cold" and sets the water level on "high." It's such a simple routine, yet Chenko loses his rhythm in the rotation occasionally. Usually there are at least two sets of scented clothes in the old locker. He amazes himself, at times, how he can screw-up something so simple shaking his head as he gets the detergent.

He pours a liberal amount of detergent on the clothes and starts the washer. The water pours in and he watches the clothes submerge and the suds form, lost in thought over a recent invoice from the treatment center at the hospital. The invoice is in an old brown folder he carries to his appointments. The folder is gaining weight. He'll carry this folder until he finds his satchel. It's a loose operation, but Chenko persists in its use, thinking its lack of everything the satchel provides will only increase the satchel's eventual return and when found, this folder will be first thing he puts in it. It will go on top of the old paperwork and he'll have the complete history of his treatment, a ship's log from one star to another.

Two other invoices have come in since the one he thinks about, he'll drag a fine tooth comb over them too, but for the moment there's a charge on the last "combed" invoice that he's not accepting, a charge of seven dollars for a straw and plastic cup. He thinks, as the clothes begin to churn and the suds begin their work. "A) I never got a cup and straw and B) I've never paid seven dollars for an empty cup and a straw and don't intend to start now." He'll go comparative on the invoice and show he can get a hundred straws and fifty cups for half the price at the cut-throat Wal-Mart down the road. If push comes to shove, he'll replace the cup and straw. It's the only option he's offering.

Chenko closes the lid when the wash cycle gains enough power to send water and suds flying landing on him and the floor. After it's closed, he places the heavy plastic detergent bottle on the lid to keep the maxed-out machine closed. He heads for the brown folder he keeps under the passenger seat of Old Red and wrestles it free.

He takes the mangled folder to what he believes is the most appropriate place for review, the john. Chenko has all the paper work, but it's not in any order. The invoice in question is found misfiled between the two new ones that for some reason have been shuffled to the middle of the stack. But it's dog-eared and easy to find. As Chenko sits in the mud room john listening to the cycles of the wash machine, relieving himself, he finds the entry in question. He looks at the address on the letterhead and knows how to get there, but it's over twenty minutes away, and decides to call the number instead.

Recordings are heard, instructions followed, buttons pressed, to get the extension with a real person at the other end. Each step increases the venom he's about to release even though he has the time to put up with the process. The music they play as he waits for his victim doesn't help. Chenko is ready to strike on how he's not accepting the charge. Ready to demonstrate in a million ways the mark-up, on something he didn't even get, as padding the bill. He'll take the approach - he's not asking, he's telling them - take it off the bill.

"Hello, this is Gloria," a voice comes on line. The voice is trained and Gloria is a professional. Chenko identifies himself and the problem. Gloria asks for some time to pull the invoice up on her screen. Chenko tells her to take her time, preparing for battle. It takes less time than he expects. Gloria comes on the line. "Here it is, I see what you're saying. It's a coding error and will be corrected." She continues with an apology, explaining the code for the cup and straw vary by one character from the code for some chemical he received during treatment.

She tells Chenko where to find the five digit codes on the invoice. "See the code on in front of CUP/STRAW is IM009, it doesn't apply to your procedure, your procedure calls for an IN009 Pharmaceutical. The correct code and charge will be made and the invoice re-issued." The correction goes from seven dollars to one hundred forty dollars. It stuns Chenko and he releases what he's been working on throughout the conversation.

The toilet is flushed; he washes his hands, grabs the folder and puts it back under the seat, through it all, still unconvinced the bill isn't padded. Based on his Wal-Mart comparison IN009 should be seventy dollars, and then starts to laugh at his crusade. He was ready to go to the mat on seven bucks and in the end got pinned twenty times over. He was ready to tell Gloria he wasn't paying for the hospital's overpriced cup and straw. The irony is not lost on Chenko; the only efficient person in the whole deal was Gloria who was very efficient in getting the hospital an additional one hundred thirty-three dollars, thanks to him.

On his way to Betty's, he's still amused by the outcome of the invoice. As his unscented clothes begin to pick up the smell of his morning cigar, Chenko thinks of the costs on the invoices. Maybe they're padded for a reason; maybe it's like what Malthus said about food, that food grows at arithmetic rate and population at a geometric rate, always more population than food. Treatment may be like food and cost like population, someone is going to starve, someone is going to die. There are more sick people than hospitals. Seems there's nothing he can do about it, nothing anyone can do about it. Just the way it is. Malthus.

Betty's is crowded, but as he enters the people in his booth are leaving. Audrey sees Chenko, lets the kitchen know and points to his booth. They exchange usual small talk, barbs and all, as she clears the table. The coffee and usual show up at the same time, less than ten minutes after his arrival. He gives Audrey a back handed compliment "Your service this morning is the most impressive thing I've seen you do in months." Audrey replies "Doesn't say much for your powers of observation."

As he eats breakfast Chenko wonders if he should tell Ilene about his crusade. He's almost sure she'll be amused by it, but after the invoice cost change decides not to. In the past weeks he's spent more time debriefing Ilene, Eve and Hope on the invoices than his treatment. It's beginning to wear thin. In his defense he really doesn't have much to tell them, he feels good, and one treatment is the same as another. But they are aware of the side effects he can't hide. He tells them it's just him and Mr. Tomb fighting. "Who's always standing in the morning?" He likes to ask.

Mr. Tomb always comes up in the end. To Ilene, Eve and Hope, Mr. Tomb becomes like an unwanted member of the family they are tired of hearing about. They want to know about his condition not some imaginary person he's trying to kill. They want Chenko to be serious with them and don't seem to understand he is being serious when he brings up Mr. Tomb. That by bringing him up, there is nothing serious to report. They don't see it that way. They know he has a history of keeping secrets. It's a paradox, the less Chenko worries, the more they worry. Their worry is the radiation or fall-out from the sixty-word bomb that will always be there.

There isn't much Chenko can do about this. So far traveling under his personal constellation has kept him and his family in fragile balance, just like the universe. Most of the effects of the impact are gone, but some still remain. Chenko deals with the ones that are left as best he can. So far under the sign he travels and the horoscope he's made, his scent has become weaker, hard for Mr. Tomb to pick up, this is what he's trying to tell them.

In the end he knows this is what really matters to them, that he can't be tracked down. For now, all who know will have to deal with the invoices and Mr. Tomb and be happy with his scent. This is the only way he knows to keep the situation less severe than it already is. All in all, he's right with the way things have gone since his confession. There is no more sneaking around and censoring the calls and mail. Enough is out in the open so he can catch his breath. As he sits at Betty's, finishing his breakfast, he realizes he isn't feeling any different now than the day he was diagnosed seven dog years ago and smiles defiantly at Mr.Tomb.

******

There comes a time when the observations of others have to be considered. There are times when those diagnosed change. No one escapes the change, some change physically others mentally and one change will precede the other, but eventually the diagnosed will experience both at the same time. Chenko is no different.

Change is a soul who wears many coats, some fit some don't. If one were alone all the time change would go unnoticed, it's the observation of others that notice change. The change in Chenko seems to fit for now. Physically he now goes un-noticed; mentally he's still wound up in the objects and people that have come into his life since his diagnosis. He's starting to talk. The subjects Chenko chooses don't go un-noticed by others.

For years Chenko has had an inner circle of friends, ten to be exact, and hardly a week goes by where at least seven or more aren't gathered at the same time around the fire, usually on Friday night, if Friday doesn't work, they find another night during the week. They're pretty hardcore about meeting up. Each has earned their own chair by the stove.

There isn't one who hasn't added to the atmosphere of their surroundings. Whatever is unacceptable at home, work, society is always acceptable at the barn; this is what the inner circle appreciates. There's always plenty of smoke and juice to help foster the unacceptability they work on one night a week at the place where it is acceptable. There is no sanctuary here for religion, politics and sex. They've dragged all through the cesspools of their minds at one time or another, with a gusto not found in ordinary men. They're all Boomers who, once a week, mentally need to be eighteen again. The forty-five or so years they have under their belt from this age not lost on them.

They're an intellectually coarse group, it's hard to get them to raise an eyebrow, but Chenko recently accomplished this. He's brought up the objects and people he's been dealing with, especially after some smoke and juice. Unaware of what he's doing. There have been times when he's asked others "What are you talking about?" while at the same time wondering how they know.

He told them of a five-foot diameter gold coin last time they were together, which in turn brought on a vigorous group discussion on the pockets in a pair of pants needed to carry such a coin and the size of your dick if you were wearing the pants and had the coin in your pocket. They think Chenko is getting forgetful of some of his best substance abuse orations. They tell him "Man! ...how could you forget last week ...'All you need in life is a pair of pants to cover a big dick and a pocket to hold a big coin. You meet both requirements 'Everything's covered.' How simple can it be? You don't remember?" This is the only change they see in him.

Subconsciously he brings the inner circle into the first two parts of his dream. If anything, a conversation over the objects and people, not to mention the Zodiac, with the inner circle will probably make no more sense than the dream itself. Chenko knows this, but can't stop himself. The trance-like orations he gives, that he has no memory of, charm the inner circle and they encourage him to keep on this new path he's found. They like hearing about the objects and people of their past, three stage rockets, Sputniks, cold wars, they've been through them all and feel obligated to give an unacceptable footnote to the history of each. They've heard of Jimmy Chesterfield and Brandsome the Handsome. Some know Donnie and the Felon.

To date, they know about the ZO and the Unknown Heaven. Their advice "Hell no, you don't want to give it to them. You want to sell it to them!" They'll all help Chenko broker the un-real deal. They're starting to get in on everything. They have no idea that what Chenko talks about is real to him. They think the exact opposite, how could what Chenko tells them be real? At times Chenko begins to wonder if the inner circle is a dream and the ZO is real. He's starting to feel an imbalance. He has no control over letting the inner circle in on his dream, just as he has no control over what he might dream that night.

All is brought on so they won't know his diagnosis, that he's ringing the door-bell on death's door-step. He still has control over this, but wonders for how long? When he confesses this to the inner circle it will be the same as telling the ZO what they want to know. But those who surround his fire are now his oracles. This way it has to be. It complicates things, now he has two discoveries he doesn't know what to do with.

He can't tell the inner circle of the discovery of his diagnosis, can't tell the ZO of his discovery of the Unknown Heaven. This is the situation; his oracles will know where the Unknown Heaven is, and the ZO will know of his diagnosis or cold war. Heaven helps him from getting the two groups confused when in a trance or dreaming. The change coming is a mental side effect of his condition. While he is not losing physically, he is starting to lose mentally, but so far this imbalance is hardly noticeable to the others. This is the change Chenko notices.

There's no point in listing the common name of everyone who goes to "Barnsville" every week. It's more important to know their "barn name." The names they carry in Barnsville are private. A name known to the inner circle, used only by the inner circle, none go by their "barn name" out on the street. Their names are similar to what one would find on a racing form at some thoroughbred horse track, and that's where the similarity ends. There's Clarence the Short, Marbles, Led Head, Elephant Pants, Smoke Eyes, D.O.A, Flounder, Juice Boy, Sneaky, Blackie (who is black), to name a few. Every member has a nickname based on a physical or character flaw agreed upon and given by the others. As a whole, the good and bad regions of their mind are similar to Chenko's.

Over the years they've developed their own dialect. If they have to describe Barnsville, they'll say it's a place covered in "beer dust," where they can go to "take the vapors" to lose "a pound of blues," it's a "clinic." To a man, each would tell those who ask, every member's mind is filled with an unknown knowledge, to the point they have to wear "no vacancy hats," each in their way capable of "ringing the doorbell of the mind." When they pull into Barnsville, they've pulled into the "car wash for the mind." This is what they'd tell you. All have the virtues and vices to be pretty good oracles, even though they are unaware this is what they are becoming.

The line between the ZO and the "Barnnites" is beginning to blur in Chenko's mind, part of the change in balance. His world is becoming a subconscious and conscious realm ruled by oracles. The last trance Chenko went into the Barnnites learned the location of the Hour Glass Constellation and the Unknown Heaven. It's in the Northwestern sky off Chenko's deck, directly over Lake Erie. He goes on about how he thought he discovered it in a dream, but it's real, he saw it one night off his deck. Saw all seven stars. The realization when it comes to Chenko scares him.

Next, he goes into Sputnik, his baking powder powered Nautilus submarine from a box of Rice Krispies, Von Braun and Van Allen, and liquid fueled three stage rockets. At the end of this trance, he asks "What ya do with a new constellation? You add it to the Zodiac or replace one that's already out there?"

In the end he leaves his oracles plenty to work on for the rest of the night. Smoke Eyes footnotes the trance with a "Wow!" then asks "Mind Bruiser, what do you see when you walk down Rorschach Boulevard?"

Chenko's oracles are no different than the ZO; they see the possibilities and power that would come behind any change in the Zodiac. Each repeats the questions Chenko has already asked himself about such a proposition. They're into the Zodiac earthquake. The evening of the last trance, towards the end, those in attendance have had enough juice and smoke to come with a first blush of the next step. It doesn't matter to them if the Hour Glass does or doesn't exist; it's going on the internet.

Here's the deal, for a fee visitor to the site can trade in their sign and horoscope for the new, improved sign and horoscope of the Hourglass. As an added option the individual can choose if their new sign is a water, fire, earth, etc., sign. There's a lot to be done on the concept, but they think they can work it out. It's a capital idea. So, it goes with Chenko and his oracles as they observe each other on this new path Chenko is taking them down.

******

The weeks roll by; the days are longer. The first seven dog years are behind Chenko and he thinks the second seven dog years will be easier. He's one-seventh of the way to his seventh star, treatments have ended for the time being and the space between scans is growing. Everything is moving in the right direction. The winter wheat is coming up turning the fields green and the odds tomorrow will be warmer than today are growing. He's like an old car with a fair body that's running well but is slightly out of alignment as it rolls over the Ohio countryside late spring, early summer.

The alignment problem has two causes. One the uneven roads and second the road debris. Chenko's routine of following his own sign and horoscope has improved the roads he travels to the locations he has to visit, but he always hits some road debris on the way. Recently he hit some large road kill and almost lost control; fortunately for him no one was on the road to catch it. It happened this way. He goes to his mail box one day, early spring and there's a personal letter addressed to him. He can't recognize the hand-writing and there's no return address. It's personal and to him, naturally he's concerned.

After standing spellbound by the mailbox for five minutes, unable to open the envelope there and get the answer to all the questions running through his mind, he instead moves up the driveway, heads into the house, goes through the kitchen and finally finds the courage to rip it open on the deck.

It's a card. On the front, a picture of a beautiful star filled sky, a navy blue back ground, holding silvery objects, framed by an eloquent bright white border. Chenko only gazes at the colors of the picture, not the pattern. Had he studied it, he'd see the Hour Glass in the Unknown Heaven. He's unaware he's been given the picture.

Inside there's no message other than the hand written note. "I know. See you on the other side. Soon." It's unsigned. On the back are a company logo and a brief note about the photo on the front, which was shot from some satellite. Lefty, Morton, Flossie and Al have followed him out onto to the deck sensing Chenko needs them there. Chenko lights a cigar and begins to inform them.

Who sent it? He begins telling them there's no doubt in his mind who sent it. He exhales with a sigh surrounded by a yellowish cloud of smoke and they hear. "Seth." He's sure the card is from Seth, but he tells the dog and cats it also could be from the ZO. One is real or was, the other isn't and he can't get the two correctly aligned in his mind, this is what Lefty, Morton, Flossie, and Al are told. Other than Lefty, Morton, Flossie, and Al, Chenko told no one about the card and its effect on his alignment. A few weeks later Sneaky and D.O.A tell Chenko they ran into Chesterfield and he told them Brandsome the Handsome is dead.

Then there's the "Barnnites." What he's told them over the winter has taken on a life of its own, even though the frequency of his trances has dramatically decreased. A week doesn't go by when they don't hatch some internet plan to market Chenko's dream, they don't want to tell the congregations, they want to sell the congregations, they don't want control they want cash. They believe they are on to something; the internet was made for the Zodiac earthquake, the Hour Glass Constellation in the Unknown Heaven. It could be a pay as you go venture for the gullible. They're out there en masse.

They just can't decide what slant they want to put on the horoscopes they'll write: religious, political or sexual. A week hasn't gone by without it coming up. The Barnnites talk enough about the scam, that it's becoming not so much a question of "if" they'll launch, but "when."

Other than the card and the scam that play on Chenko's mind, late spring, early summer has its positive side. The hardware he's making for the vanity is turning out better than expected, he's completed the first of seven handles, he has the look he wants and the rest will be easy. Ilene and he made time for a long weekend. It was nice and what is needed, but the weekend is not without its surprises.

It was the weekend of Seth's funeral, that Chenko had no knowledge was taking place. That weekend he and Ilene were at Moccasin Lake. After hearing about the funeral and that Jimmy Chesterfield was upset with him for not showing, he doubts he would've come back for it, had he known. They had clear skies, the cottage on the water, a pontoon boat and were really getting in touch with each other. That weekend he was more into saying "hello" to Ilene than saying "goodbye" to Seth. Knowing wouldn't have made any difference. The weekend with her was that good.

The first surprise that weekend comes by land; they get a better cottage at the same price, because the one they were supposed to get has plumbing problems. The second comes by water. They're on the pontoon boat after a romantic morning that drifts to a new reality when Ilene brings up

Chenko's side of the garage. The morning makes the conversation possible; she was going to take advantage of it. As she begins Chenko takes a long pull from his rationed beer and wishes he had a cigar. "Nye, when we get back home will you do something with the far corner of your side of the garage?" Due to the morning, it was a more a request than a command and she asks in a way that the right response could lead to a romantic afternoon on the boat.

Chenko answers her with "Sure." She knows it's his sincere "sure" and gives him a big smile, but feels compelled to go on. "I was back there the other day looking for a place to put the extension cord for the Christmas lights and there's a beat-up old tarp on the floor I know you don't use any more, a broken step ladder, why? A bunch of old paint cans ready to catch fire, and your nasty gym bag, it all has to go," her tone becoming more normal than romantic. Chenko is too stunned to comment, all he can do is nod, lost in what she's just told him.

Ilene is tempted to ask "Did you hear me?" but doesn't, she's too lost in his glazed eyes and instead asks "What? She has no idea of what she has just returned to him, but is aware something she said flipped his switch.

Chenko doesn't try to explain; she doesn't like the satchel, never has, instead he takes advantage of his look and asks if she wants to go skinny dipping. For a moment she considers it, but they're not the only boat on the water. "They can't see us," Chenko explains. "Binoculars," she answers "Ever hear of them?" He smiles. "Not going stop me."

His tee-shirt and suit are off in a matter of seconds and he dives into cold late spring, early summer waters of Moccasin Lake and comes up in the sunlight. Chenko floats uninhibited on his back, a fountain of water spouting from his mouth. When the stream ends, he's back to coaxing Ilene, but she's not coming in. She meets him halfway, slips out of her suit and puts on his tee-shirt offering to dry him off when he comes aboard.

Chenko floats in the water with a million thoughts running through his mind. The agenda he set from the start and how it's changing. The finances are handled, part of the family knows, but not all the family or any friends, and the way the scans are coming back the heroic act is still out in the distance. The act of disappearing like the old or badly wounded Indian who wanders out into the cold winter woods and is never seen again, the noble warrior who won't put those who love him through his pain and suffering in the end. They don't need to be around when he can no longer fight off the wolves and bears. Chenko smiles as he swims to the boat, the heroic act is at seventh star distance. The return of the satchel helps.

With the passing of the first dog year Chenko is not concerned about the second dog year or the dog year after that or any of them. The ZO and the Barnnites will always be there as long as the treatments last. The diagnosis and treatment have created them. His alignment improves as he accepts there will always be dreams and oracles under the constellations.

CHAPTER V: FATE

F ate is like giving a box of matches to an arsonist, one doesn't really know what they'll do, but one has a pretty good idea. Fate is neither kind nor unkind, it's like water and fire, it can relieve your thirst and keep you warm one moment or drown and burn down all that's around you the next. Fate doesn't care. Fate is just something out there everyone has to deal with; it can't be controlled; only survived. It's something everyone thinks they understand, but can't. If anything, it's like God, someone you don't really know, but meet in the end. This is exactly what Ananias Zachenko would tell anyone. He doesn't pay much attention to fate.

Mid-summer of Chenko's second set of dog years finds him looking for Linwood Sharlitin. Through the winter snows and spring rains he hasn't heard from Linwood. He could try to call Linwood, but this isn't the deal. Linwood is to keep in contact, not disappear. Chenko doesn't care about the money or the dresser, he cares that he's been played. It bothers Chenko that Linwood would think he's someone he could take advantage of. It's like Linwood has him confused with someone out of the basement of General Grade School. It doesn't sit well.

The situation with Linwood is good and bad. It's good in terms of side effects, aches and pains have leveled off so Linwood replaces them as Chenko's major concern. At the very least Linwood takes Chenko's mind off these problems. It's bad in terms of the dark regions of his mind Chenko is beginning to explore. He knows vengeance is the Lord's job, but there are times he feels he should help out.

There's a line Chenko has drawn in his mind, it's based on what his father once told him. "I get along with everyone until they give me a reason not to." In Chenko's mind this is a fair line and has served him well, but once this line is crossed, conscience takes a back seat to revenge. Linwood has crossed that line.

Chenko walks into his office at the barn one day, not unlike some sheriff out of the Old West, has a bottle of Dickel in one hand and a shot glass in the other. He sits down at his desk, pours a shot and throws it back, pours another and sips it. He leans back and places his feet on the desk, lights a cigar, and looks out the window.

A golden wheat field fills his view, running flat for a quarter mile and then up a gentle slope, another quarter mile, to the tree line. There the color changes to different shades of green from the leaves of old and young trees. From the inside all he sees is gold and green, but the view is deceptive; he knows outside its hot, dry, dusty and bright enough to bring on a headache. This deception only adds to the thought of tracking Linwood down and he reaches for the false bottom box, takes the cards out and nothing more. In the future he plans to saddle up his iron pony and ride Linwood down. He'll hit both hideouts and give no warning.

Linwood doesn't want to be captured by Chenko; he's fallen into that category of someone Chenko might not release. There are many reasons Chenko feels this way, none are legitimate enough to merit what he's beginning to plan. But for one reason or another, Chenko has developed an attitude towards Linwood filled with bad intentions. He sips on his whiskey and thinks of capturing Linwood on a humid day, the part of the day when the mosquitoes begin to swarm, sundown. Take him to woods, take off his shirt, tie him to a tree, and cover what's exposed with sugar water, leave him there for a while, check back on his work around midnight.

This plan didn't just come to Chenko; he learned it in the Army. The war games in basic when they were in the field for a week. The guys going over, in a mock battle with the guys who just came back, the un-skilled versus the skilled. It was the big operation towards the end of basic, squads, platoons, companies, battalions, everyone was part of something, and everyone was in the field carrying rifles, machine guns and mortars loaded with blanks. Everyone got to hear what might rip through them one day if they didn't pay attention. Everyone was into small unit tactics, driven by the five paragraph field order defining mission and objective, how to take over or take out a target.

The first two days of the operation the new guys found that being captured by the old guys wasn't such a bad deal. If one got captured, one was taken out of the exercise and for the most part put in a field where one could spend a couple hours sleeping and smoking, until someone would ask what they were doing over there. After the morning of the second day there was a run on the real estate in the field. To the point the brass told the old guys they better make it so the new guys don't want to be captured. It wasn't a problem for the old guys.

By sundown of the third day, they started pulling the new guys out of the woods. When you got captured from that day on, they took off your shirt and the laces from your boots. The captive found a tree between them and their boot-lace tied hands and, when secured, got doused with a special canteen containing a couple of packets of sugar from a C-ration mixed with water. They showed the new guys how to use the terrain, for example, the endless army of insects they could get on their side. They knew how to create a hostile environment.

Even those who managed to scrape through their laces and escape weren't without their wounds, and everyone's back had more than mosquito bites. Chenko saw some pretty nasty backs, swollen hands and bad allergic reactions; one guy got bitten by a copper head. Those captured by the hundred-and-first had a complimentary "101" scratched on their forehead. It was starting to get real. Things changed after that day. It was pretty Junior Varsity compared to what the old guys were capable of, but enough of a lesson, that when Chenko went over, he went with the attitude of saving a bullet for himself if it came to being captured.

Chenko toys with the idea of getting hold of Linwood's shoe laces while locked on the view of the gentle slope leading to the tree line above it. The dog days of August were coming, maybe that would be the time to strike. Through it all, the thought of the sugar water treatment isn't as bad as what he saw on the other side of the pond. It wasn't like he was planning to tie Linwood to the back of a Jeep and drag him a few clicks down some rough road to get him to talk.

A host of ideas are running through his mind on how to deal with Linwood, none of them are good and all come from bad past experiences. In Chenko's mind Linwood has become the objective of a mission Chenko won't abandon. He gets up from his desk and heads for Old Red, in a week or so he plans to ride down on old Linwood. There'll be no stopping him.

******

A few nights after the decision is made to track down Linwood, Chenko sits home alone in front of the TV. Ilene is at a meeting for one of the charitable organizations she belongs to and before she leaves makes one request of Chenko "Nye, make sure you are here when the guy from the high school Speech & Debate team drops off the frozen pizza. He left a message he's coming by."

It's a fundraiser for the team, and they know the Zachenko's always buy a pizza; they've had their number for a long time. Chenko responds with a theatrical sigh "Yeah." Then he footnotes "The Athletic Boosters will be by in another month." He'll be right; the Boosters also have had their number for a long time, only they'll be dropping off raffle tickets.

Mr. Thorndyke pulls in the driveway about ten minutes after Ilene leaves. He gets out of a new black high-end BMW with vanity plates that read "Thorny." He's just finished a round of golf at the prestigious Oakley Country Club that will come up during his brief conversation with Chenko, along with what he shot. Under his arm he has a ten inch frozen pizza that will relieve Chenko's wallet of thirteen dollars.

Chenko sees him first, catching him pulling in the drive from the living room window while making his way to the mud- room john. He decides to take a leak before answering the door; while he's in the process he hears the doorbell more than once. Mr. Thorndyke has been to Chenko's house before, about two years back he delivered a pizza. Mr. Thorndyke is an 'A' personality type; he's not one who likes to be kept waiting. The more he rings, the more Chenko takes his time. Chenko recognizes him and wonders when his kid is going to graduate.

When Chenko leaves the mud-room john, he decides to walk through the garage and come up on Thorny's blind side to get the drop on him, like it's the Old West and there's some big rancher on his range. He pulls it off just the way he wants, giving Thorny a small shock with his pleasant "How's it going?"

Thorny wonders how Chenko got behind him. No one was around when he came up the driveway. Thorny spins around from the front door towards the voice and begins to answer how it's going with where he's been and what he's been doing.

Both walk towards each other as they talk. Thorny is dressed to the 'nines,' everything matches and is expensive, no one would doubt he just came from the country club. In comparison, Chenko has on an old Harley Davidson tee-shirt Hope got him when she was in Vancouver, a pair of well-worn jeans and sandals; he looks like he works at the country club, yard gang.

Their small talk goes back and forth; Chenko listens more than he talks, being made aware that Thorny is an import guy. It's not as if Thorny doesn't have some good traits, it just seems they hardly come out during the conversation. Thorny is okay, but not a guy Chenko would hang with, he's no Billy Kaloon, who also belongs to the club. Chenko drops Billy's name and Thorny is somewhat surprised and impressed Chenko knows him. Thorny finally hands Chenko the pizza and then asks "Next year, what do you think Fifteen dollars?" Chenko smiles and answers... "I'm thinking new phone number." He hands Thorny a twenty and tells him to keep the change. It forces an extended, but sincere thank you from Thorny. He gets in his car and he leaves not knowing what to make of Chenko.

The frozen pizza makes it no farther than the kitchen counter; Chenko is distracted by Lefty, needing to go out and the headlines in the newspaper next to the pizza. He reads a short article about a guy falling through a false ceiling, "breaking and entering" some pharmacy in Akron. It was quite a drop and the guy will be in the hospital for a while. The story is an ironic piece, pointing out in the end; he'll be getting the painkillers he was after, but not the way he planned. He then cruises through the sports page, reads an opinion on the "excessive celebration penalty,' agreeing with the conclusion – "act like you've been there before." He then puts the sections of the paper back in order for Ilene who has yet to go through it. He lets Lefty in and heads for the TV.

He slides onto his Lazy-Boy and grabs the remote and goes to the channel listings. For the moment there's not a program that interests him, he'll have to go through them again. Chenko has no idea how many channels he has on the cable and begins to count, quitting after thirty. It's not like the old days when there were only three black and white stations out of Cleveland. Chenko remembers when stations advertised some programs were in "color."

When he and Ilene have told Eve and Hope about those days, they act like he did when his parents told him about radio – What? No picture? Only now Eve and Hope ask – What? No color? For a moment Chenko thinks how information and entertainment have evolved from one generation to the next, first being heard, then not only heard, but seen, then seen in color on more stations than one cares to count from everywhere.

There's absolutely nothing on and he begins to surf the channels, blowing by most, but stopping at some for as long as ten minutes. There are the reality shows revolving around tow trucks, pawn shops, salons, kitchens and people stuck on some remote island, housewives in big cities, arrogant chefs in some kitchen, and bad girls in some club, just to name a few.

These shows all follow the same formula based on conflict; someone scheming, and then arguing, then the fight. The producers are betting the viewer wants to see the outcome. They set the hook by making the schemes wilder, the grudges deeper and the outcome more dramatic each week. The shows hold the viewer's fascination for a period because they try to make unacceptable behavior the solution. They're deceptive; one thinks the situations are real when actually they're staged. The cost of staging the production paid in public humiliation. Sometimes it takes as much as ten minutes to figure this out.

There's also a ton of infomercials that suck up some time. For anyone losing their hair, getting fat, sexually dysfunctional or in need of more money, there's no shortage of information, too good to be true, on how to solve these problems. There is always something that will go on a viewer's head, fold-up under their bed, keep their zipper down and pockets full. The best are the nineteen dollars and ninety-nine cent items we can't live without, and "But wait there's More!" These are Chenko's thoughts.

It doesn't matter what channel Chenko is on when he decides to go back to the kitchen. A dormant appetite is starting erupt; it's been a while since he's had a snack attack and he smiles. It's like the old days. As he walks to the kitchen, he begins taking an inventory of what he thinks is available, more in the mood for something salty than something sweet. He gets no farther than the pizza thawing by the paper.

He reads the instructions on how to cook it. It's a nice-looking pizza, with a lot of cheese and sausage, but there are no microwave instructions. It's a problem; Chenko lost his stove privileges long ago. Ilene does not want him on any part of her range. In fact, Chenko is a disaster in her kitchen. And she's upfront about it being "hers." For the most part Chenko respects her wishes; he knows he's always eaten well in her kitchen. The only appliances he's allowed to use are the toaster, refrigerator, the microwave and he's always on the edge of losing the microwave.

It is like the old days, he's hungry. Chenko is hungry enough to gamble and walks over and begins to study the range and its unfamiliar controls. He presses some controls for the oven and next thing he knows is 450 degrees pops up digitally on some screen by the control. He thinks to himself this sounds about right and opens the oven door to feel if this was enough to get the heat build-up. It's there and he removes his hand, closes the door and looks for a cookie sheet. He finds one in the third cupboard he goes through and wrestles it free, unwraps the pizza, puts it on the sheet and throws it in the oven.

Finding and setting a timer never occurs to him, he looks at the kitchen clock and makes a mental note to be back in fifteen minutes. He returns to his chair and watches a show about people's houses filled with garbage and another show about pythons invading the Everglades, they caught one eighteen feet long, he watches until he smells the pizza burning.

The smoke build up isn't bad and Chenko gets to the pizza before it becomes totally inedible. He pries it loose from the burnt cheese welding it to the sheet and slides it onto a large serving platter he finds in one of the three cupboards. Ignorant of the fact it's one of Ilene's "special occasion" platters and his good fortune she's not there to witness all that is going on in her kitchen. He puts the sheet back into the oven, he'll clean it later. He opens some windows and hopes the smell will be gone by the time Ilene gets home.

Some napkins are grabbed along with some iced tea and he caravans back to the TV. When he gets there, they're starting to dissect the eighteen-foot snake and the show isn't going to go well with the pizza. He moves on and three stations up stops, locked on a guy he feels he's seen before, only he doesn't know where or when.

The guy is selling buckets of food so one can survive Armageddon. He's been around a while and has a history. Actually, Chenko has seen him before, but is unaware; he and "a" wife have been on TV for years. At one time he had a wife who looked like she spent a lot of time in front of a vanity. He has another wife now and it's hard to figure out what she's spent a lot of time in front of, but whatever it is, it isn't an improvement. Chenko listens to them both as he crunches through the pizza. He has the feeling he and his first wife never made any sense and it's no different now with his second wife. It's as if he knows this guy's history, but doesn't know when or where he picked it up. Chenko has seen him before in his dream, but doesn't make the connection.

Chenko sits spellbound by the guy, his wife and two other guys (who look like they've consumed a warehouse of the food buckets), one guy sings and the other guy explains the deals at the bottom of the screen. They got a deal on the buckets ranging from twenty dollars to three thousand dollars. After listening to them for a while, it doesn't take long to figure out if they don't have *Isaiah* from the *Old Testament* and *Revelations* from the *New Testament*, they wouldn't have much to talk about. And that somehow these books and the Bible were really written to get one to buy food buckets, as many as possible. That's what it's all about.

The camera pans to the small audience, what one could consider as lost souls. They sit around tables and sample the food. Naturally it's the best food they've ever eaten and each thank the ones up on the stage for giving them the opportunity to be brought in on the deal. They're all behind the idea of being able to out run Armageddon, somehow, they think what they're doing makes them look smart, chosen. It gets to the point where the snake dissection three channels down start to look good in comparison. From all Chenko has heard about Armageddon, he seriously doubts anyone can out run it, no matter how many food buckets one has. On top of that, Armageddon comes from a dream, the dream of John.

Just as Chenko picks up the remote, the camera pans back to the audience one last time and there he is, Linwood Sharlitin, sitting in front of this guy somewhere in Missouri or Tennessee, one or the other, Chenko heard both states mentioned through the show. One may be the state of some "prayer warrior" mentioned. It doesn't matter. There he is sampling and commenting on a bowl of lima beans. Chenko is captured by him; he freezes, dropping the remote like a gun.

It is Linwood all right, slicked back hair and all. Linwood can't believe what he's eating and Chenko can't believe what he's seeing. The banter between Linwood and those on the stage praise the product. After paying a lengthy tribute in praise to the product, Linwood quickly gets a plug in for The Everlasting True Vine Ministries back in Ohio. The guy on the stage gives him just enough time to get this in and then directs him back to product praise. Chenko misses the part where Linwood proclaims he's the shepherd of the flock, too lost in all he's seen and heard about a bowl of lima beans. He also misses the part when Linwood tells the guy, his wife and the two fat guys, he has purchased three thousand dollars' worth of product; too lost in the fact the product has become their god.

Gradually Chenko begins to slowly move his head up and down and no longer sees Linwood. What he begins to see is the tree line outside his window at the barn. He begins to wonder when Linwood will be back in town, vowing when he finds out, Linwood will enter a little basic training for Armageddon. He wants to make sure when Linwood gets back, he'll enter a hostile environment. When Chenko finds out his share of Linwood's purchase and the "new" Ananias Zachenko the environment will go from hostile to "deadly."

Before Ilene comes home Chenko goes through six more channels that have the same type of guy. One guy, according to his calculations, puts the spear Goliath carried, when David dropped him, at seventeen and-a-half feet long, almost as long as the python three channels down, Chenko thinks. Another is talking to some alcoholic in his TV audience, telling the alcoholic he doesn't need to worry about a thing, because he just healed him. One wears the five stars of a general on the collar of his black shirt and has a gold cross emblazoned on the shirt pocket against a very busy background, letting all know he's the guy God put in charge of their soul. All beg in the name of God.

All have books and CDs that will clear everything up, all have product. All have a phone number and some partner of theirs one can talk to, who'll straighten everything out according to one's financial support. All they have is free - with a love offering. He's seen every one of them before and every one of them makes Chenko uncomfortable. More uncomfortable than Ilene makes him when she smells her kitchen, sees the platter, finds the cookie sheet and learns the pizza isn't in the refrigerator, but in his stomach.

******

Except for the night of the pizza, when he caught Linwood and the cast of soul-chasers on TV, for the most part, since the return of the satchel, it's been smooth sailing for Chenko. He has less to put in it than when he started. The satchel is now always in Old Red and never leaves the cab; it's tied down behind the passenger's seat, right over the jack. All he has to do is hit the lever and pop the seat forward, unzip the satchel and grab the folder or put it back. The folder leaves the cab, not the satchel.

The satchel is at a third of its capacity. On top of the folder of medical records (his star log) another folder will soon be added. The satchel has been found, but not the dresser. This is next. Chenko unaware finding the two fulfill a set of requirements he set early in the game for more time. Past thoughts about time are now dormant in his mind.

Linwood is back. At the rear of the Everlasting True Vine Ministries, he unloads a shipment of food buckets for resale to his congregation. The next step will be to change the contents of the buckets so they're not technically the same as what he purchased. He'll alter them in case his supplier gets wind of what he's doing and a legal problem pops up. Linwood believes he can pull off a one hundred percent mark-up. In another day or so, he'll have new labels to wrap around the buckets letting his flock know who is really giving them the opportunity to be prepared for the end.

After stacking the buckets, he goes to his office to do a little paperwork, making sure the cost has been spread correctly over certain members of his ministry who are still unaware they are members, his twelve new financial disciples. Chenko's portion is two hundred fifty dollars.

Initially Chenko becomes aware of the charge when he checks the month's financial activity. The transaction is on a card both Ilene and he use. It's not the biggest charge on the statement, but it's far from the smallest. It looks like something Ilene charged, and at first glance Chenko doesn't pay it much mind. It's not his, so it must be hers.

It's a while before she asks Chenko why he charged two hundred fifty dollars for food buckets when she goes online to pay the bill. She reads the line charge to him, giving date and origin, her face a giant question mark. When she finishes, it all starts to fall together for Chenko and he tries to explain he didn't make the charge, but keeps to himself who he thinks has, he just tells her he'll take care of it.

Ilene doesn't like his answer and presses for more details, but he tells her again, it's a problem he'll take care of; but his short answer doesn't answer the "why" as far as Ilene is concerned. He should have gone with the standard "I don't know." But he does know.

The only other comment he makes to her is "Someone has made a huge mistake." The threatening way he says it is enough for her to abandon the topic. She thinks the tone is directed at her, but it isn't. She's been down the road before with him whenever he uses this tone of voice and it often leads nowhere. She'll pick another time. Chenko is fortunate she's not in a mood to peruse the issue. His dark side forces him to keep secret who he thinks made the charge and how he'll take care of it. He's now thinking beyond sugar water. Ilene doesn't need to know what's going through his mind.

Ilene, still uncertain about the mystery charge, reluctantly pays the bill anyway. But the charge isn't a dead issue. Chenko says to himself he has a month to get a two hundred fifty-dollar credit on the next bill to make it a dead issue. He hates the thought of all the calls he is going to have to make and immediately fines Linwood two hundred fifty dollars for the inconvenience. A fine he has every intention of collecting. His next move is to build a folder on Linwood, starting with the statement giving the when and where Linwood really stepped over the line and it will always be in the satchel. The folder with two cards stapled on the inside left flap. There's the statement, two cards and a brief write-up with the approximate date and time he caught Linwood on TV. Linwood is going to pay for the calls in spades.

Chenko has set a picture in his mind of Linwood pulling two hundred dollars out his wallet along with another hundred dollars for the dresser and doing it in a willing manner just to get away from the madman in front of him. Chenko goes through his repertoire of head games to bring this about. However, an incident that involves Chenko, the Barnnites and the whole community pops up out of nowhere and temporarily puts his mission on the back burner.

******

Shortly after the discovery of the mystery charge on the statement, an incident occurs. Sidetracking the deadly mission Chenko wants to put in operation towards an objective he no longer wants to take over, but now wants to take out. Linwood temporarily drops off the radar.

It is early Saturday morning when Chenko gets a call from Marbles. He stumbles out of bed and grabs his cell from the pocket of his pants on the hamper and answers. "What!" Next thing Chenko hears is: "You better get down to the barn. Cops are here, so is the paper, TV is on the way." Marbles doesn't tell Chenko anymore about the situation, he's known Chenko since they were two. To give him more details would just delay what needs to happen, Marbles feels he gave him enough and hangs up before Chenko can ask anything.

The sun has been up for less than an hour, it's early for Chenko, who's not a morning person and he wrestles on his clothes, hoping not to wake Ilene, hoping he can leave a note. His wrestling match doesn't go unnoticed and she asks "Who was on the phone? Where are you going?" She's been awake since his terse "What!" Chenko answers with two words. "Eddy. Barn." He's not tearing out of the house, she reasons, but he's up and going, which is out of the ordinary.

Ilene knows the early morning is not the time to go into detail with him; she knows who called and where he's going. That what was said in less than ten seconds, is important enough to get him to move. It's enough; eventually she'll find out what's going on and has no problem going back to sleep.

Old Red and the cigar fire up at the same time and Chenko runs a variety of scenarios through his mind with the information he has. First is someone broke-in and took his bike. Took off and somewhere close to the barn, he and the bike are spread all over the road.

The second is somebody dumped a body by the barn. Someone set the place on fire. He has enough scenarios to last the trip to the barn; more keep coming as he moves through the extremely slow-moving traffic. When he finally makes the entrance, he gives up and concludes whatever is going on is big. At this point all that holds his attention are the vehicles and people on his property.

All the Barnnites are there, Chenko is the first to know, but the last to arrive. Along with the Barnnites are an equal number of people Chenko doesn't know standing in a group in front of his office window. A policeman stops Chenko. Chenko explains who he is and parks in front of the first set of double doors.

His oracles surround Old Red and before getting out Chenko has the window down and leans out of it waiting for someone to speak. Nothing is said, they wait for Chenko to get out and point to the gentle slope of wheat below the tree line. When Chenko begins to take it in, Sneaky tells him "Got three cop cars on the place. Those people up by your office, well, they're the media. Everyone is looking for you. They're starting to think you and the rest of us are involved. You know, did it...What we going to tell them?"

After Chenko hears this, in light of what he sees, he laughs in amazement. He then thinks for a moment and tells them "Maybe we did" as the angle to play, but knows there may be some truth behind it. His oracles begin to think of the past winter. Chenko continues "We're just a bunch of fucking geometry geniuses. Want to tell them that...Who wouldn't believe us?" It's obvious to every Barnnite the better question is "Who would believe us?"

What all see, with the sun coming down on the slope at a perfect angle, letting the shadows bring out its intricate design, is a "crop circle." It's large and complex. It has a central theme held by a frame of elaborate geometric designs involving both curves and angles. The media's cameras are going off like machine guns, to capture every curve and angle. It's an incredible work of art.

There isn't a Barnnite who can't read something into the design given the conversations they've had over the winter. All feel like they're in some *Twilight Zone* episode. Inside the sophisticated frame there's a circle about one hundred feet in diameter, inside the circle appear seven, seven pointed stars that if connected by an imaginary line would give the pattern of a "Z" or an hour glass.

The circle, with the stars, sits within a vertical and horizontal axis that has a line at a forty-five degree angle starting at their intersection. The line meeting the edge of circle closest to the origin of the axis and then it is picked up again at the same angle on the farthest edge of the circle from the origin. An intricate arrowhead design, the type found on the needle of a skillfully built compass, is at the end of the line, it points to the northwest.

Some of the Barnnites say the design says "ZO," the Z pattern inside the circle or O. Others think it's a map pointing to the Hour Glass constellation, Unknown Heaven. All begin to exchange their ideas of what the circle means and there is no shortage of views. Led Head comments the design would make a nice tattoo, suggesting every Barnnite get one to commemorate the occasion.

******

Garlin Mears stands in the midst of at least five reporters in front of Chenko's office window. Garlin owns the field and pretty much all of the southwest corner of the township. Over the years there hasn't been a Barnnite he hasn't had a conversation with. Knows them all, individually or as a group, they've never given him a problem, other than some of the thoughts they've shared with him.

They always call Garlin "GM," he likes that and if he were twenty years younger, he'd probably be at the barn every Friday. He knows Chenko the best and certainly wouldn't miss any opportunity to paint Chenko, or anyone of them into a corner, just for fun. He's a wily old boy, part of the Greatest Generation, landed at Anzio before he was twenty and did the early to mid-Forties touring Italy, came home went to work and bought a big part of the township. People listen to him.

GM was in the "Big One." Chenko got on GM's good side the day the Anzio prayer came up. GM sets the stage telling Chenko "It got so bad they were handing the cooks rifles. One cook was heard praying. At this point in the story Chenko breaks in and tells GM "I know, God come to Anzio, you come. Don't send Jesus. This ain't no place for kids." He tells GM he heard about the prayer from a chaplain when he was in the "Long One." It impresses GM.

The Barnnites begin to light up around Old Red and for a moment their exchange of thoughts turns to coffee. Everyone wants some, but no one wants to wrestle with the grimy coffee maker in the barn. The traffic running by the barn makes this the only option. Sneaky is chosen because he'd be the only one who would clean the pot before using it. Everyone knows this, including Sneaky. He agrees because he's low on smokes and this would give him a card to play as the day goes on.

As they wait for the coffee, the past winter is reviewed, there are a lot of statements that start out "Remember when Chenko told us about" and some fact about the ZO, the Zodiac Earthquake, the Hour Glass constellation, large coins and purple backgrounds is recalled.

Chenko isn't involved in any of the conversations, he's too busy watching GM talk to the media, eventually pointing Chenko out to them without any hesitation. As they all start walking towards Chenko, he interrupts his oracles conversations and announces "We got company. Let's all put on our thinking caps."

They reach Chenko and his oracles at the same time Sneaky brings out the pot of coffee and Styrofoam cups, setting the pot and cups on the tailgate of Old Red. Although it appears that GM and the media are expected, the coffee happens by chance, and in truth no Barnnite wants to share it, but they do. Sneaky bums a smoke, grumbles under his breath and goes back to make another pot.

Before introductions are made, GM makes an opening statement to his media friends about the group giving them the coffee. "I certainly wouldn't rule these guys out!" He gives Chenko and his oracles a wink which could be taken as a green light to have fun with the media, knowing from past conversations what each is capable of. GM doesn't like the media, never has. It becomes their inside joke. GM, someone people listen to, implying they did it. Chenko shakes his head, smiles at GM after the set up and they wait for the questions.

The questions never come, because at that moment the professor the media called at the start of the day rolls down the drive in an unmarked police car. The car is followed by a beat-up late model Toyota Civic occupied by three graduate students who will operate the measuring equipment stuffed in the trunk. It's Professor Mandrake from some small college down in southwestern Ohio along the Ohio River. He is Ohio's leading authority on the phenomena.

Mandrake approaches the group gathered around the tailgate of Old Red and introduces himself. "Dr. Mandrake, and before you get started let me say a few words. This isn't my first crop circle." He's a short stocky guy who looks more like a truck driver wearing a lab coat and holding a clipboard than a professor. He's in his early fifties and would rather work his clipboard and assistants recording measurements and radiation than talk to them. Dr. Mandrake tells them "I know what to look for, but you have to give me a chance. I'll tell you what I find."

He pours himself and his assistants some coffee, thinking it was made for them and begins a brief lecture he's given more than once. "First ones showed up in England, 1980 around Stonehenge in an oat field. Their distribution is growing; not only England, but France, Canada, Australia and the U.S. have experienced them. Eventually every country will experience them. In 1990 over one thousand were reported. The frequency is growing. A way to distinguish the true from the false is the condition of the crops used in the pattern. In the true circle, which is yet to be explained, the crops are just bent at the base and not damaged, the field comes back in few days as if nothing happened. Circles with damaged crops are far less intricate, eventually explained and the culprits known. Here in Ohio the Serpent Mound down around Brush Creek has been a target, along with Miamisburg, West Union and Paint Creek. They first showed up here in 1996. We plot the positions of the constellations at the time of the occurrence to see if a pattern exists, to learn the 'position of occurrence." It's my theory there is an association with their occurrence and the movement of known and unknown constellations." His last statement spooks the Barnnites.

A helicopter appears hovering over the circle, moving from one location to another, taking aerial photos. The chopper is directed by the graduate students on the ground working a radio frequency to give the pilot the altitude and direction for the picture to be taken. Dr. Mandrake comments "This is the most elaborate crop circle I've seen in Ohio." It's not hard to see everything about it impresses him. Everything he has already said and is about to say, is recorded. Chenko flashes for a moment to his dream and sees the ZO writing down what he's saying. The similarity of what he dreamt and what is happening not lost on him.

The helicopter is privately owned. Its flight was set up by the media in conjunction with Dr. Mandrake. Their choppers were on other stories and they went down a very small list of people who owned helicopters in the vicinity, made some calls and lined up Gus Fratelli. Gus is another story. As fate would have it Chenko, Marbles and Blackie all know Gus from school. During a radio transmission Gus hears Chenko's name in the background conversations. Gus transmits back "Wait a minute, is there a guy named Chenko down there? Put him on!"

The student looks at Dr. Mandrake and tells him "Gus wants to talk to someone named Chenko." Chenko doesn't expect this, but steps forward, Dr. Mandrake nods and Chenko is handed the radio and begins with a "Yeah?" The pilot, in a long delivery, giving Chenko time to recognize a voice from the past, asks "Is...This...Ananias...Zachenko?

It's enough to let Chenko recognize Gus' voice and he answers "Roger that. What ya think of our work?" He has set the stage and direction. After Gus quits laughing, he answers "Any other name, but yours, would be a surprise. You're at the center of this?" Chenko answers "Everyone is at the center of something." Chenko and his oracles begin to go on record.

Next thing Gus hears is a question blurted out by one of the media "You think these guys could have done it?" Gus's words are barely understood against the background of his own laughter as he answers the question "Oh, there's no doubt." Knowing what he's seeing, there isn't anyone he knows on the planet capable of making what his chopper is over.

The media are inclined to take Gus' words, rather than what is implied in his statement, this along with what GM implied is starting to look like a story, Dr. Mandrake at one end and these guys at the other end. They couple together "I wouldn't rule these guys out." a direct quote from the land owner, with "Oh, there's no doubt," a direct quote from the pilot as a starting point. They've got a cast of characters to work with, they're looking for culprits or answers from Dr. Mandrake. It's a good set up.

Gus talks to Marbles and Sneaky. The conversations are total nonsense, like Chenko's and Dr. Mandrake is annoyed and directs the radio back to his student. A few more instructions are transmitted and chopper disappears. Dr. Mandrake walks toward the crop circle and all begin to follow.

Halfway to the slope below the tree line he stops and informs all, from this point on only he and his students would be going to the "site." He and the students will be at the site for at least a half hour before they report back.

There's some discussion on this, to the point his students put their equipment down, but in the end all reluctantly agree. It would be enough time to get the camera's rolling on the Barnnites, one reporter for every two Barnnites with a half hour to kill. It gets to the point a group picture is taken for TV and the papers. When Dr. Mandrake and the students return, they're asked what they know about the Hour Glass constellation and Zodiac Earthquake.

******

There isn't a Barnnite who will back away from the idea they're involved and there isn't a person in their right mind who wouldn't say, once they saw the crop circle photo and the group photo "No way!" Each knows this, so why not play it? People love to overlook the obvious. Each is good with their reporter, just stopping short of a confession. Each plays their part well for a group on their way to becoming an urban legend.

If the radio transmissions annoyed Dr. Mandrake, the questions aggravate him to the point he ignores the questions and tells the reporters the wheat is bent, not broken; in short there is absolutely no way that those who may claim credit are responsible for what he has found. He has a clipboard of data to back up his position and issues a challenge to those responsible to repeat the circle the following night. He was pretty clear that the odds it was made by anyone one in Ohio, let alone the group the reporters were always pointing to, were about the same as the odds of getting hit by a meteor.

Two stories unfold that day. The Barnnites and Dr. Mandrake's made for interesting listening, viewing and reading. But it hits the streets first, Ilene knows all about it by the time Chenko gets home, his name along with others heard first at the supermarket. What is heard on the radio, seen on TV, read in the papers, icing on the cake.

It becomes more humorous to others than to her, but for the most part more lean toward genius than idiot when the topic comes up. Her only comment is "Nye, you can make the unreal real. I'm thinking that's dangerous. It's a gift, but the wrong gift for you. It's like the ivy." Chenko laughs and nods in agreement, seeing himself on a bench in front of Betty's.

The Hour Glass constellation, the Zodiac Earthquake, the ZO, more interesting than the facts and figures from Dr. Mandrake, he becomes background to a story some believe, but most don't. In the opinion of most, the Barnnites would be at the top of their list of the "least likely" to create what they've seen. However, from the day of the crop circle on, Chenko, his wife, kids and those who were there, are amazed at how many people believe the Barnnites pulled it off.

They're no way close to a majority, but they're out there. No Barnnite has backed away from their assertions. Considering the work they enjoy the association. But more than this, Chenko is amazed that portions of the second part of his dream have been recorded, filmed, written down and fed to the public. There is also no way to overlook the perfect alignment of the crop circle with his office window as mere coincidence. All his amazements lead to new thoughts about the third part of his dream, the dream to come.

******

There's a large sycamore tree in the Cuyahoga Valley that is the exact age as Chenko. It's seen its share of harsh winters, summer droughts, lightning strikes, blights and infestations, but for the most part has a pretty good life and is surrounded by its children. The sycamore sits near the bottom of a steep winding road. The road's navigation, going up or down, requires caution.

The wise travel it at a safe speed. The caution of others has always been the ally of the sycamore. It's within striking distance from the road, but has never been hit. It doesn't go unnoticed by the wise traveling the road, its appearance more appreciated than feared. Many have stopped to carve their initials into its base. It's one of the parks "sweetheart" trees. Within a few days Chenko's mission will put him at the base of the sycamore twice.

The initial impact of celebrity wears off in about week. But a small part of the effect will always remain; there will be a constant trace of radiation from the crop circle. It's now part of the local history. As fate would have it, Chenko and his oracles are the source for half of this history. In the years to follow the event will be remembered in late July conversations taking place on picnics and in beer tents, something for the young and old in this part of Ohio, home of the Zodiac Earthquake.

During the week following the discovery, Ilene teases Chenko about some of the comments he made to the media. She likes to strike randomly "Tell you what Nye; I've seen some pretty advanced Michigan teams handle the Buckeyes." At first, Chenko will have no idea what she is talking about, but it becomes clear as she goes on. Ilene and her cubs never miss an opportunity to put a zealot like him in his place. She begins "Oh how soon we forget," then continues with Chenko's direct quote "It doesn't surprise me Ohio has more circles than Michigan, Ohio is more advanced."

Chenko made the comment off the cuff, after one of Dr. Mandrake's remarks concerning the distribution of crop circles in the Midwest and it made the paper. Chenko is not alone; the other Barnnites are subject to the same treatment by those close to them for the comments they made. They've all been called ZO-heads, Hour Glass Boys and Zodiac Zeros. The treatment comes with the territory they all seem to want to claim. None of them mind, they'd do the same if the shoe were on the other foot.

The news of the crop circle and its impact isn't lost on Linwood, what better time to advertise a revival and move some buckets. Thank You, Lord! He knows the pictures in the paper and on the internet can be used to tip the gullible souls over the edge and into his hands. The work shown, as well as those who may have created it, are subject to all types of interpretations.

What else can it be, but a sign? Linwood knows what kind of sign it is and it isn't good. People are going to have to be warned and then prepared. He turns on his laptop and begins to create his advertisement. Compliments of the Barnnites, there are no shortage of mysterious terms like the Zodiac Earthquake; the word "oracle" appears in articles, along with a few other key words of similar nature that can only have their origin in the dark side, way he sees it. The Barnnites have left behind plenty of ammunition to point at the anti-Christ and the End Times. Thanks to them, he's well-armed to go after the people he wants to capture.

Below a downloaded picture of the circle, his fingers fly across the keyboard "God Has Told Me to Warn You About This Wheat Field. The Reaper Is at Hand. Prepare." Linwood goes into the body of the ad urging all to obey his special anointment. He brings up *Revelations*, the Rapture, becoming one of his prayer warriors to avoid what is coming and a litany of other terms used by those in the business. It's written with the naïve in mind, as an opportunity to make them look smart by not ignoring his anointed warning. Everyone will look dumb, but them. He knows his audience. It's written for those blind to the fact this is a one-sided opportunity and they're the target. His warning goes out under ETVM.com to the media and charged to one of his financial disciples. Chenko will escape this charge.

As Linwood prepares for revival, Chenko prepares for revenge. When the crop circle disappears, Chenko returns to the barn and his mission. He looks at the tree line outside his office window and makes maps to both of Linwood's locations. They are close enough to be hit on the same day. A route is developed to the targets in Barnsville Township. It will be a nice ride for Jack (the name of his bike) and him, give him plenty of time to scheme.

As he looks at Jack, he begins to think of "battle-dress" and the gear he'll take. It's like Halloween; he doesn't get to dress up that often. For the most part Chenko keeps an acceptable appearance, has all his life; in fact, at times, he's been complimented on his attire and the way he looks, thanks to Ilene. As a general rule his opinions are in his head, not on a tee-shirt. But there have been a few occasions, based on situation, when he goes into character and can appear to be someone he isn't.

For the Linwood situation, Chenko decides to go with his "out of town" look and this look is far from choirboy. He decides on his blue "Insane Clown Posse" tee-shirt, with clown faces that not only scare kids, but adults as well. His jeans will be held up by his big buckle belt, the buckle in the shape of a skull. Big buckled belts are intimidating; those who've been around them know when pulled free of the belt loops, wrapped around the hand a few times, it can be a nice weapon. The weight of the buckle can accomplish a lot.

He'll take the switch-blade he brought back from the war. Maybe take it out to clean his nails while talking to Linwood, like he did when talking to prisoners. The heavy boots will be on. He'll wear the black and gold knit hat, pulled down to his eyebrows, so when one looks at him the first thing they'll see is "Hidden Rocks" in gold thread written across his forehead. He'll wear the eighty-dollar sunglasses, and never take them off in Linwood's presence to keep it on the dark side.

The only drawback to the appearance Chenko is after, is his lack of ink, he doesn't have any tattoos. Other than this, he has the dress and gear he wants for the mission. It will take at least a day to find the shirt and belt. They're someplace in a closet, dresser or chest, tucked away out of Ilene's view. It's been a long time since he's worn them. The shirt is a gift from one his "hoodlum friends," as Ilene likes to say and he bought the belt before they got married. Chenko has known from the moment she saw both, first chance she gets, they're gone, but he's pretty sure this hasn't happened yet and he can find them. The shirt and belt are like Ilene's "Special Occasion" platters, only brought out when needed.

He begins to wipe Jack down. He cleans the mirrors, chrome and painted surfaces, Jack sparkles in the light of a clear day. Chenko gets on and fires Jack up. He gets off, lights up a cigar and listens to the bike. It sounds good and as much as he tries to hear something that isn't right, he can't.

Ever since the Canal Fulton tune-up, with the exception of a plugged rear tire, everything on and in the bike is perfect, been that way all summer long. A new rear tire is suggested, but Chenko believes he can get one more season. The bike makes him feel good and for a moment he thinks about his illness and concludes he's running like the bike, since he's been back to the shop. Alone, in a moment of total reverence, he bows his head and thanks the Lord.

The following day Chenko finds the shirt and belt, it takes a big part of the morning. It's time consuming putting everything back just like he found it in the closets, dressers and chests. He does a less than perfect job; the time spent posing in front of the mirror would have been better spent covering his tracks while in Ilene's territory.

The condition all are left in is enough to raise some questions and comments from Ilene when she gets home. All to be asked and made when he gets home, whatever he was looking for he should have asked her first - instead of leaving a wake of destruction in his path.

She's suspicious; whatever he is looking for, is probably hidden from her. Also, he will probably tell her what he was looking for is something he knows she's already thrown out. She's ready for anything. Maybe he's slipped something by her. She wants to know what; she's prepared and can't wait for him to get home later.

The cigar and Old Red fired up; Chenko backs out of the driveway muttering "Won't be long now," in reference to the third part of his dream, not Linwood. He reviews the previous night's dream and finds nothing, but feels the third part is at hand. It's an uncomfortable feeling, but one he'll have to deal with as he makes his way to a clean Jack. It's strange and he has no reason to feel the way he does, but the feeling can't be stopped. He finds the time to scheme on Linwood is being taken up by the dream.

It's a hot, humid day, the sun is out, but it's hazy. Chenko fires up Jack, puts her in gear and heads out. At the first stop light he knows the "out of town" look is working, he fills the rearview mirror of the car in front of him and can see the old driver's eyes are locked on him. His smile isn't enough to make her break contact. He's polite and doesn't rev the bike, and begins to think maybe he's gone a little too far with the look. She acted as if she had seen "Public Enemy Number One" in her mirror. Chenko thinks maybe it's the shirt.

Chenko moves in and out of the traffic, he likes cranking the gears and feeling the bike respond perfectly to his every move. He's on the edge of reckless, but he's gliding at high speed with full control, just the way it's supposed to be. He's making better time than expected and decides to pull over and grab a quick lunch. The way he's dressed his options are limited. He drives towards a place coming up the road with some bikes in front of it called "The Buzz." He's been by it before, but never in it.

If it weren't for the lunch time crowd Chenko would be back to the dream, but he gets involved in a conversation with two of guys at the bar dressed in similar fashion to him, only their shirts have skulls. It's a horseshoe shaped bar, Chenko and the two guys have the corner by the restrooms.

The two guys are trying to figure out what the "33" means on a bottle of Rolling Rock. Chenko can't take listening to them any longer after placing his order for the 'Weed-Buster Cheese Burger" and a bottle of Rock. He likes the green bottle. Rolling Rock is always his "road beer," it's not like he doesn't know its history. He waits for the right time to interject, not interrupt with... "My guess would be the '33' is for the year Prohibition ended."

The two surprise Chenko with their reply after the right time comes and he fills them in. One says "The end of the Volstead Act," the other says "Repeal of the 18th Amendment," in agreement to Chenko's comment. The conversation grows, the two are like Chenko, not what they appear to be and three beers later all have said all that needs to be said to clear up the "33" on the bottle. Including that Mississippi was the first to outlaw alcohol in 1907. "Mississippi!" One exclaims. The other sighs, "Twenty-six years without a drink, not Mississippi!" ...and slams half his Rock back as if there were a chance someone might take it from him.

Each has bought a round, Chenko backs off the start of another round. He tells his new friends, Bud and Larry, he has some place he has to be. Another conversation starts to unfold. Chenko tells Bud and Larry he's going to Left Behind Antiques. Bud and Larry, almost at the same time, tell Chenko "That's Kenny Bruce Sharlitin's place – it's not open." Chenko tells both he doesn't care, he's going anyway. Bud and Larry just shake their heads; no one wants to see Kenny Bruce. It's not enough to stop Chenko. He tells them the way he plans to go and Bud and Larry point out a shortcut.

Bud asks "How well do you know the valley?" Chenko nods. "Read the hat." Both know someone from Hidden Rocks would be familiar. Larry jumps in "Turn right at the next intersection, instead of going straight, keep your eyes open, it's not much of an intersection."

It becomes a race between Bud and Larry who can get the next word in. Larry edges out Bud "There's a carved-up sycamore by a road you want to turn left onto." Neither one needs to go any further; Chenko now recalls the place they're talking about. The Ivy incident didn't happen too far from the sycamore. Before he can wave them off, Bud jumps in with, "Go up the winding road, a half-mile on the top is the Left Behind and the world's biggest headache." Chenko smiles at Bud and Larry. "Thanks"

Chenko catches the intersection and makes the turn, everything moving like it should and the sycamore comes into view. As he moves towards it, he comes up with a novel idea totally foreign to any idea he's had during the day, week, month or year. Aware he has a nice size knife with him, he's going to stop and carve Ilene's and his initials in the tree. He has time, no one's expecting him at the Left Behind, and this won't take long. It's a good idea; one day soon he'll take her to the tree, she'll like it. It's a really good idea and he brings Jack to a stop at the base of the sycamore, gets off, pops the blade and goes to work.

In a half-hour his work is finished, he spends another ten minutes looking at the tattoo he's put on the sycamore from every angle. He does some touch up work, satisfied it's better than most, moves on. Chenko reaches the top of the hill and within a half mile pulls into the Left Behind. Jack comes to a stop and Chenko looks at an old run down house, with a cinder parking lot scratched in front of it that could pass for the house in *Psycho*. "The Bates Motel" he mutters and isn't surprised.

Kenny Bruce appears before Chenko can get off the bike, seemingly out of nowhere. Chenko speaks first "I'm looking for Linwood Sharlitin." Kenny Bruce, in a terse voice, replies "For what?!" The reply pisses Chenko off and in low seething voice tells Kenny Bruce "For a while."

The conversation doesn't get any better. "That's your fucking problem," Kenny Bruce tells him. "It's yours now," Chenko fires back. The meeting goes downhill from here.

Chenko gets off Jack and lights a cigar while staring down Kenny Bruce and waiting for what he'll say next. It's a play he feels he can make, Kenny Bruce is big, but in all the wrong places, and although he looks older than Chenko,

Chenko knows he's not. His clothes are dirty, finger nails long and black, hair thin. It doesn't take Kenny Bruce long to figure out who the alpha male is and in a blast of bad breath shouts out. "Go to the Everlasting True Vine." Chenko shouts back, "What!?" Kenny Bruce backs away from Chenko like a cat giving up territory. "Up the road. He runs the place. Now get the hell out of here!" and puts his right hand in the pocket of his overalls. The move is enough to make Chenko not want to test what might be in the pocket and he leaves.

There's no way to tell if Kenny Bruce is telling him the truth. For a moment he thinks about going to the second location like planned, but then decides to give it ten miles up the road before he turns back and heads to the second location. He didn't expect a third location.

After eight miles he spots the sign for The Everlasting True Vine. The sign is impressive and the empty parking lot is paved and large. Chenko parks the bike as close as he can in front of the double door entrance. Sits on Jack and looks at the tinted windows that allow those inside to see outside, but doesn't allow those outside to see inside. He revs the bike a few times to see if he can get anyone's attention.

No one comes so he drives to the rear of the Everlasting True Vine. It's as nice in the back as it is in the front, paved with a nice shipping and receiving area. The area looks like new work. An office door is open and as Chenko gets off Jack and heads towards it, before he reaches it the figure of a woman fills it.

As he gets closer, she begins "Thought I heard a bike." She's middle-age and not hard to look at and seems more attracted than repelled by Chenko's appearance. She tells Chenko she's Roxanne, ETVM executive secretary. "Looking for Linwood Sharlitin," Chenko tells her in a pleasant voice.

"Any other time, but now, you'd have found him, he just left, but he'll be here all day tomorrow. Want to wait?" she jokes.

Chenko likes her flirting ways and follows her back to the office; he'll leave an unsigned note. Once in the office, he writes on a Post-It note "Be seeing you real soon!!!" Roxanne comments that it looks like it's written in an angry hand, a lot of hard angles make up the words.

Chenko smiles like it's meant as a joke and tells her to make sure Linwood gets it. She nods and then begins to talk about Linwood just stopping short of how'd she'd like to break away from him, she seems open to any opportunity. Chenko doesn't say much, scratches his face with his left hand so she can catch his ring. She doesn't seem to notice.

As she goes on, Chenko begins to casually look at the surroundings, waiting for a polite way to end the one-sided conversation. The surroundings are nice. He sees the open door from the office to the bathroom, but it isn't until he takes a few steps to his right that he sees the second bathroom door leading to a bedroom that looks like it's just recently been used. He takes one more step to the right, still pretending to listen, to catch more of the room and sees his dresser in a far corner. He's found the dresser.

******

As fate would have it, Chenko is two doors away from what he has dreamt, but they are closed. One door to the waiting room, another to the auditorium, where he'd find a large gold coin that seems to float in front of purple curtain, above an Altar. It's just as well these two doors are closed; there would be no telling Chenko's reaction to the sight. Fate might be doing him a favor. But here's the thing - if Chenko is ever asked "Did you ever make it to the actual 'site' of a dream?" Chenko will answer "No." But the truth would be "Yes." Doesn't matter he's totally unaware of the truth.

The fact the dresser is in Linwood's bedroom triggers a silent rage Chenko can barely keep under control. He abruptly nods to Roxanne to end the conversation and heads for the door, but she follows him out still talking as he starts Jack, he leaves her with just a nod as she' starts telling him she really likes his bike, wants on. All Chenko thinks is he can go home now and plan tomorrow, no need to go to the second location.

Going down the winding hill to the sycamore beyond thirty-five miles-per-hour is pushing it. But Chenko is feeling the bike even though the terrain is against him. Driving down the hill feels like a challenge he can handle, like his illness. He never really knew what happened. Rear tire might have blown. Might have hit some wet leafs. Whatever, Chenko and Jack fly off the road. They're airborne for about ten seconds before hitting the sycamore. Jack bursts into flames and falls to base of the tree, the fire finds the sycamore and goes to work. Chenko bounces off the tree and is dead before he hits the ground. The second time he's at the base of the sycamore.

Ilene never gets to ask the questions she has waiting for him. Never gets to see their initials. The satchel and dresser were found. And there is no third part to his dream; the shortcut takes care of it ever happening. Chenko has his illness under control and then this. What about all the dog years? Just no way to explain it, other than this is the way fate works. Fate doesn't care.

CHAPTER VI: DIMENSION

These three dimensions: length, width and depth make up the physical universe. They are used to fix a body in space, to give its position. This is what is known of the physical universe. But there are also unknown dimensions in other universes which determine more than position. Everyone will enter a universe of unknown dimension in the end and for everyone this universe and dimension will be different.

Chenko pulls himself from his broken body and stands next to it. It isn't a spontaneous poetic move, more like a prize fighter, knocked down for the first time, slowly finding his knees, then his feet, eyes blinking and wondering what just happened, unaware he's been counted out, still wanting to continue. Upset the fight is over, especially when up to the final blow things seemed to be going his way. He was winning.

He's shocked beyond all comprehension when he figures it out. Immediately feels he's the victim of something he sure as hell didn't see coming, sucker punched by Mr. Tomb. This can't be right! But knows it is and there's nothing he can do about it. All he has to do is look down at the mangled body at his feet to know the truth.

In a moment of sheer terror, he almost laughs out loud at the absurd thought - he's never done anything like this in his whole life - which he now knows has just ended. He can't get over it. A lot of people will be surprised, but none will reach the plateau of "surprise" that he is on - ever. This, by far, surpasses any surprise he had in life by an unbelievable magnitude. He raises his head up from the lifeless body and watches the flames from Jack consume the sycamore, wondering what's next, having no idea what to expect.

Chenko has entered his dimension. He's aware nothing will be the same from here on out, or so he thinks, but some things will. All the thoughts he's ever had on being dead converge into one thought. He's amazed at how he can recall his earliest to his latest thought on death. Every one of them is in the correct order and crystal clear, moving at the speed of light towards the final thought. And the final thought comes to him in unbelievable clarity, unlike any great thought he had in life.

He knows now, but doesn't want to accept the fact. Even with all its clarity what he imagines is pale in comparison to what is about to happen. He'll find out the body at his feet is like the skin a snake sheds, no longer of any use. Everyone spends three days in their dimension (Tomb). This is not by chance. These days can seem like seconds or centuries. They're like dog years, they're arbitrary. How long the days will seem depends on one's soul. The dimension is not eternity. It will end and then eternity begins. Unlike life, where you have to be born again, in this dimension you have to die again.

In this dimension the good and bad one created in life and had no knowledge of is made known to them. The blood donated and the life saved; the person you mistreated and the life you ruined, for example. Chenko will find the senses of sight, sound, taste, touch and smell remain, along with all his emotions, joy and sorrow, love and hate. There will be memories of those left behind and those who've already passed through this dimension. Their memories will allow something new. Right now, there are two of him at one place, but this will change, soon he'll be one again and able to be at two places at a one time, if he wants. This will take a while for him to realize.

The ground view of Chenko, mentioned in the very beginning is over. This is the aerial view. This view will determine which region is greater, the good or bad that occupies Chenko's soul. What region will carry over into this dimension? Like everyone, he'll have the opportunity to influence this final view by how he travels through this dimension with those who share his "death day."

In the beginning a piece of scripture mentions strangers and angels. There will always be strangers and angels, take Emmett the angel. Emmett is assigned to me and the closest match I have to Chenko. We're both from eternity and sent to you by the One who rules eternity. To let you know what is in this scripture is true.

Emmett comes to earth to smoke. He does this by choice, not command. During one of these breaks, he met Chenko. It's a long story and probably best told later. For the time being, let's continue with what has just happened and what is to happen. Emmett, with two "m's" and two "t's" as he likes to say. Other angels like to joke around with him when he says this, asking if the "M" and the "T" stand for "Empty." It's like he already has a barn name.

******

The emergency crews arrive. One crew puts out the fire; the sycamore, like Chenko, can't be saved, the other crew polices up the body, which is a mess, all agree it will be a "closed box" funeral. His shirt is soaked in blood; the evil clown faces will never be seen again. His buckle, blown off on impact sent flying into the woods, won't be found for many years to come. The upper left quarter of his head is missing and it's stuck to the sycamore, part of his brain being cooked by the flames Jack has created. Chenko sees it all. It doesn't seem to bother him; it's nothing new. He's seen mangled bodies before, just not his.

Both crews agree the site is good enough to make the news (which it does) and take their time, so as not to miss the arrival of the news crew, the third and final crew to make the scene. It's definitely a three-crew wreck. They all know the emergency here was over the second this clown hit the tree, this isn't an emergency, and this is clean up. They all agree it had to be fast – a flash – about the only good fact they can point out to each other as they clean up the mess.

Chenko can move about and tries to talk to them, tries to let them know that it was fast, but more than fast, it was shocking beyond belief. He tries to tell them, tries to touch them, but they can't hear or feel a thing. It isn't what he hoped for, but is what he expected. It's a whole new ball game, with every move he makes he learns something new, something different.

As he watches the crews and hears what they say, he thinks of Ilene, Eve and Hope, his brothers and sister, all his friends and begins to cry. His tears burn, creating more tears, he's blinded by them. He makes no movement or sound, just tears. What has he done to them!? The thought brings on more tears. He's never cried like this.

The pain of separation more than he can bear and part of the dimension he's now in. It has to be overcome by others he will meet on the road he's now on and the places he'll now go. For now, a past will exist, he will never forget them and they will never forget him. They will see each other differently now, maybe in a memory or dream, nothing more.

This dimension, however, is not without its benefits. After a while Chenko begins to gather himself, his eyes clear, his vision returns. He feels washed by his tears. Thoughts are coming and going beyond gigabyte size, in real time and his processing ability is keeping up with all the information. On his best day in life, he never processed the amount information he's processing now. On top of this, there isn't a circuit board in his mind even close to a blow-out. It's all getting through.

He's beginning to handle the power of the input and output process to his advantage. Soon he'll learn how to use the power to give others an advantage. He can keep the power to process to himself or share it with others. Choices still exist in this realm. This is an important lesson to learn in this dimension, some learn it, others don't.

A feeling comes over Chenko that it has to be later than it is. The sun was going down when the news crew wrapped up the story, but for him it's still the middle of the afternoon. It's as if the sun and the moon fill the sky at the same time. He sees them drive off in darkness while still standing in the sun. Time is standing still for him and he can feel it. The sun is going down for them, but the sun isn't moving for him. He'll learn the trick of getting out of this dimension will be making time move once it has stopped - like now.

He puts himself in Ilene's and his bedroom, sitting on the corner of the bed and waits for her. The phone rings, a message is left, Chenko listens. It's unbelievably painful. When it ends, he begins to work on what to say, even though he knows she won't be able to hear him now, he knows someday she will and he'll tell her again. This is not a feeling he has, but a knowledge he gains. What he will say is for down the road when they meet again.

It has to be perfect. He'll start working on it now, this moment. While he's sitting on the bed, he also starts walking down the road leading to the "ivy incident" and out of the valley to his home. Walking to a place he's already at, unaware he's doing this. Something one can now do in this dimension.

As he walks there is nothing unfamiliar to him, he knows where he is, everything is like it was when he started the day, except he's pretty sure he's dead, but now holding out for a bad dream. Maybe it's a dream; he's had dreams before that seemed real, but knows in his heart of hearts this isn't a dream. This is an important development; it allows him to take notice of the things around him.

He can throw a stone; it leaves his hand, but never seems to land. He can see the shadows of the trees on the road, but not his. When he stands next to the stream leading to the pass he once defended, he sees the reflection of the clouds in the sky, but not his. He is and isn't in the physical world. He's dead he concludes and it's like popping a boil, after the pain the relief.

He thinks to himself "I know the year, month and day of the week, but not the date. It's either August thirteenth or fourteenth, 2012." He does a calculation in his head with amazing speed and perfect clarity to determine it's the thirteenth, he adds the eighth month, thirteenth day and twelfth year together and comes up with thirty-three and for some strange reason laughs.

Bud and Larry flash through his mind for a moment, but they leave as fast as they show up. Next a green bottle flashes by, disappearing just as fast. And without explanation Chenko blurts out "Should have told them the age Christ was crucified." He also had that knowledge at the time. It's as if he realizes he made a mistake, this is the real information that should have been given, that this is the information that now matters.

Somehow this realization eases his mind and he wonders where Christ is and tries to figure out what is supposed to happen next. Chenko figures he'll run into Him any minute, but has no idea now, what a minute is, now that time is standing still. He continues to walk towards the bedroom he's already in. As he sits in the bedroom, he begins to tell Ilene "I'm walking towards you, always."

******

Emmett sits on a rock around the bend. He will be the first being Chenko meets in this unknown dimension. When Chenko comes upon him, Emmett says "I really dig your threads." It's not what Chenko expects, not at all. Emmett continues "Name is Emmett, two "m's", two "t's", call me 'M T'." Chenko is too caught up in how he's now dressed and misses the introduction.

Chenko now has on his favorite tank top with "Barn-Fest" written on it, over that is his favorite shirt, unbuttoned, a Hawaiian shirt given him by his mother-in-law, and tan cargo shorts, given him by his girls for Father's Day. On his feet are tire tread Ho Chi Min sandals.

M T waits a few moments for Chenko to look up, knowing he didn't catch a thing after his comment about Chenko's threads. He'll introduce himself again after Chenko gets over the shock of his attire.

It's like hitting the sycamore again. All Chenko can say is "Jesus!" M T decides to treat Chenko's exclamation like it's a question and answers "Maybe. What do you think?" M T likes to play a lot of visuals on those who cross his path. Right after he asks the question, he takes on the look of a beat-up homeless person in worn out clothes who has the clearest eyes Chenko has ever looked into. If they weren't the eyes of Christ, they were the eyes of one who's seen Christ.

Chenko doesn't know what to believe. Next M T tests Chenko and asks him for a smoke.

Chenko, like he has all his adult life, instinctively reaches for his smokes and they're in his shirt pocket, like always, and hands M T a cigar. Somehow, it's already lit as he hands it to him. M T takes a huge hit and the smoke he exhales is the whitest smoke Chenko has ever seen and has the smell of the best tobacco ever created.

Next M T takes out a deck of cards and starts doing amazing card tricks while answering Chenko's questioning eyes and addresses his exclamation "Nope." He reintroduces himself right down to the two "m's" and two "t's." He ends the introduction with "You don't remember me, do you?" This time Chenko answers "Nope." M T replies "Good. It will work to your benefit in the end. Thanks for the smoke."

What M T says confuses Chenko becoming as much a riddle as the card tricks. He instructs Chenko to look in his shirt pocket, telling him to hold onto the card he'll find there; someday someone will ask him for it. Chenko pulls out the two-of-hearts. "Don't ever lose it." M T says, smiles gets-up from the rock he's sitting on and heads to the side of the road, sticks out his thumb. As he does this he adds "You're not where you think you are. Be seeing ya."

A car, the likes of which Chenko has never seen before, comes down the road and picks M T up. The driver is someone Chenko knows well, but try as he may, he can't place him. Both are gone before Chenko can yell out in amazement "Hey! Wait a minute!" He hears M T yell back in a laugh that is almost infectious "What's a minute? What's a dog year?" It's a clue to the riddle.

Chenko sits on the rock left vacant by M T. It's like finding the stool in his corner and once on it, getting a huge hit of the smelling salts to bring him back. Once on the rock everything comes back to him in perfect clarity. It all started with his diagnosis and his decision he wasn't going to be part of the lost patrol in the war of procedure and coverage. He lights a cigar and remembers when he thought he'll save face by the way he ends the game. He did save most of his face, except for the quarter cooking on the sycamore. That's what will be remembered. He has to laugh at himself, how the end did come. No doubt his end will be remembered now, his and the sycamore's. It's like a phone conversation he once had regarding a bill, the outcome totally different from what he planned.

The thoughts keep pouring in. He's in the spot where he learned the three phases of doubt: when he had no doubt, was filled with doubt and then the doubt was taken away. All his doubts have been taken away now. He knows what just happened. He sees himself in Billy Kaloon's office, at the same time he sees himself waiting for Linwood Sharlitin in the barn. In Billy's office he's telling himself he's not going anywhere until the satchel is found. At the barn he's telling himself he won't be going anywhere until the dresser is sold.

Technicality the dresser isn't actually sold, in that Linwood never gave him any money, but is with the fact it's in Linwood's bedroom. Chenko would've gotten the money, this will be treated as a fact and over rules any doubt. So, it's sold. He'll find this dimension is not without its technicalities.

What he's coming up with is the fact that after the diagnosis he built a case for more time around a satchel and a dresser. He found the satchel and technically sold the dresser and by doing so ran out of time. That was the deal. At the time he had no idea his search for both would lead to this. The realization of these two events unfolding the way they did a perfect example of how strange life could be.

None of it technically makes any sense. Seems between the satchel and dresser, were diagnoses, the calculations of dog years, people from the past, dreams of oracles, constellations and unknown heavens, stems of the plants that were bent, not broken, to give an unbelievable flavor to the time spent searching for a lost satchel and dresser. Had he known, he would have abandoned the search.

The very things he thought would give him more time gave him less. True, he is dead a little over a year after his diagnosis, but it wasn't from what he expected.

Then fate stepped in and he met Mr. Tomb in the form of a large sycamore. He concludes all he really has now is a past life in a new dimension and moves off the rock. After he gets up there won't be any part of his life, he won't be able to recall and the sun above him slowly begins to move.

As he continues to walk towards the bedroom, he's already in, he begins to hope Ilene won't have to identify his body that she can be spared this. He hopes the unpleasant task falls on one his brothers somehow. As hard as it would be for a brother, Sonny or Jeep would be better than Ilene.

He hasn't forgotten how to hope, as in life, hope is a big part of this dimension. From the corner of the bed, he continues "I'm walking towards you, always. When I come into view, you'll see me as I am, not as I was." Hedging his bet in case what he fears comes to pass. Later on, he'll find out it turns out as he hopes. All Ilene has to identify are his wallet, lighter, and switchblade.

******

Just like birthdays one shares their death-day with others. The number of souls who die every day is an estimate, based on a rate, the actual number is only known to God. Man can come very close to calculating the number on occasion, but the actual real number only God knows on every occasion, by the second, minute, hour, day, week, month, year and some other measures of time we have no idea exist.

Death, the great equalizer, knows no religion, race, country, language, wealth; all the things that mattered in life don't matter in death. The fact of life is no one gets out alive, as all find out. Other dimensions know a death beyond our comprehension, but still determined by which way the scale tips.

Good and bad deaths exist in the dimension Chenko is in. In his past life he was told he had to be born again and proclaim it, in this dimension being born again is more than a proclamation. In this dimension it's found out if you *were* born again. If you never proclaimed this, you're subject to technicalities. If you said you were born again and the good in you outweighs the bad there's nothing to worry about. If you said you were born again and the bad in you outweighs the good there's plenty to worry about. The way you carried your weight in life is the weight you carry to other dimensions. Death in this dimension is the weigh in for eternity. Some make the weight, others don't.

Chenko continues to walk through the valley. The familiar is starting to become unfamiliar, but not in a disturbing way. There are roads with no traffic and roads with plenty of traffic, there are trees and brush on the sides of some, houses and buildings on the sides of others. What Chenko now experiences are surroundings that are very similar to places he knew in a past life, and his past life begins to become another life filled with memories of good and bad. He comes upon a place that in another life is Betty's. He knows it isn't, but knows it will be like Betty's. He'll go in.

He can't feel himself breath as he walks towards the place and wonders how long he's been walking effortlessly without feeling his breath. He lights a cigar, like the old days. The smoke pours from nose and mouth like always, but he still can't feel himself breathing and wonders if the smoke is an illusion. There's no ash as the cigar grows smaller with each hit. It's different and better than the cigar he had on the rock. He doesn't have to flick it into the atmosphere like he used to, when his thoughts were held by three stage rockets. When he's finished with it, it disappears. It's a nice feature of this dimension.

The place is crowded. Everyone has one thing in common they're all dead. All trying to come to grips with where they are, all dressed in their favorite clothes. Some sit in booths, others tables. All died the day Chenko died, but at different times.

At one table there's a suicide bomber surrounded by his victims, at another table a drunk sitting with the family he killed. Mothers hold aborted babies; fathers watch over abused children. In the booths there are those who lived a good life and had a noble death.

Every type of death that took place that day, from every part of the planet is represented at a table or booth, the old and the young. Most were victims of the four horsemen: war, pestilence, famine, and disease. Some are victims of the fortune fate provides, others the victims of time and natural causes.

Everyone speaks the same language in giving their forgiveness or planning their revenge. There are whispers and shouts. Chenko can hear every conversation, but more than this, he can understand every conversation.

It will take Chenko a while before he understands this is a huge part of this dimension. In this dimension is a language he's never heard, but yet can speak. Though all speak and hear the same language in this dimension, some understand all that is said, others don't.

He finds a booth and takes a seat. He looks around to see if there is anyone he recognizes. His gaze is met with smiles, vacant stares and threatening gestures. A waitress comes and asks "The Usual?" She then smiles. Before Chenko can answer, she leaves and returns with coffee. Chenko is interested in what she will bring and answers her question, "Sure," and returns the smile. He takes a sip of his coffee and is overcome by its taste.

"Okay," she says "First look into this mirror." She pulls a compact from her apron and holds it so both can look into it, all they see is the reflection of tables and booths. While she does this, she mentions the compact was the last thing she put in her purse the day she overdosed. She pulled it from the center drawer of a large maple vanity in her room. "Wonder what ever happened to that vanity?" she wonders. Chenko begins to process.

He leans back and looks at her. "What's your name?" She answers "Jazz - Jasmine."

"Jazz what's up with the mirror?" Chenko asks. It doesn't surprise him that neither saw their reflection; he wants to know why it seemed to be required. "Some sort of Vampire thing?" he continues. Jazz smiles and explains, "Every once in a while, a live person shows up in here, they're lost in a memory or dream... They're in here looking for someone, when they show up in the mirror, we have to let them know the memory or dream is over. You're good. I've been waiting for my mom, so I can get out of here. Not that I mind this place, but I'm ready to move on."

She's waiting for her mom to have that over powering memory or dream and show up in her mirror. She doesn't want to miss her. It's almost like listening to a pretty young waitress explaining her hopes for the future that once occurred in another life.

Jazz brings the usual and Chenko eats the two poached eggs, bacon, cup of fruit and rye toast, it goes down like a Thanksgiving dinner. As he eats Jazz begins to clean up the tables by his booth and they begin to talk, each tuning out the conversations around them. Jazz tells him of a life that started out right, took a bad turn and wound up all wrong. The words are few, but through the new language they now speak, Chenko can feel the pain that was a big part of her life.

It's her choice to stretch out her three days in the tomb. She's waiting for her mom who bought her the vanity, who tried to make it as good as she could, but Jazz wanted the boom of the fast lane. Through it all her mom was always in her corner. Jazz wants her to come to this place, show up in her mirror and tell her she's fine and loves her and move on. Before she can do this her mom has to know how she feels. How she has always felt, even in the worst of times, she needs to let her mom know of the love that is and will always exist.

Chenko processes the time he came across a vanity. He begins to describe the vanity to Jazz; with each word she becomes more excited. She's in total agreement with everything he's describing, the large mirror and six drawer pedestals, the soft yellow maple finish, the burn marks from cigarettes that missed the ashtray. He describes the hardware, but doesn't tell her he replaced it. He doesn't tell her it's had several finishes since she last saw it, that it had been kicked around for a while and that he found it at Goodwill, that Goodwill saved it.

The vanity went through several rehabs, like her. Like the vanity, she too moved from one place to another, each place worse than the place before. One day she went into a lingering coma from her overdose; no one could pull the plug on her. It took her a long time to die. She finally died the morning Chenko hit the sycamore, but actually died the day she stuck a needle in her arm. Chenko tells her "It fell into my hands in another life." I know right where it is. It's like brand new, like when your mom got it for you. Be brand new for you and your mom when she shows up too."

Jazz believes him, because he levels with her, telling her "Seems you gave everyone a lot to get over. When they do, they'll come," Chenko continues. "In another life hope was lost and found like a coin, in this place 'hope' feels like a coin that's always in your pocket." Jazz smiles at him and asks "Will you be back?"

"You bet," Chenko answers, smiling. "I'll come to your kitchen again." Chenko does come back, on many occasions, just like he did go to Betty's in another life.

In the bedroom the sun begins to go down. Chenko hasn't moved. Chenko would've bet the pocket he puts his hand in is empty, but feels a coin. He looks at his yard and Eve and Hope playing in it, the sand box, swing set, their friends, parties. He watches them grow up in front of his eyes. He hopes he's left them the strength to overcome what has happened and rubs the coin in his pocket. It's a very slow and pleasant sunset.

He continues with what he'll tell Ilene in a soft whisper "I'm walking towards you, always. When I come into view, you'll see me as I am, not as I was. I have a coin in my pocket for you."

******

The moon appears full and bright. It's like a flashlight in the sky. The sky is clear and like looking into Emmett's eyes. The sky blends into a far-off horizon that gives the promise of something beyond the dimension Chenko is in.

There are no stars or constellations to wonder about. All that exists is the light of the moon showing the clarity of all the things it falls on. The light of the moon and vast clear, spotless sky, beyond any night Chenko can recall in another life.

After leaving "Jazz's kitchen," Chenko finds himself walking on a road with trees and brush on both sides. At first the trees are full, their branches strong and bursting with foliage. The underbrush is made up of grasses and wild flowers moving in harmony with a gentle breeze in the moonlight.

As he continues the scenery gradually changes: most the trees have been wounded, their branches broken, some are dead, some are dying, others just surviving, none are flourishing. The brush gives way to the thorns and weeds in constant conflict with all that surrounds them, always trying to overtake the ground of others. The light of the moon wrestles with dark clouds that appear out of nowhere and the obstacles in front of him can no longer be seen.

It becomes dark enough that Chenko picks up a small branch and has to feel his way down the road like a blind person whose cane is their eyes. For a moment he thinks of turning around and heading back to the kitchen and waiting for morning to come. The advantage of the light in the sky is gone, no matter which way he decides to go, forward or backwards. It's an uncomfortable feeling either way and he decides to continue forward, hoping the clouds will disappear as fast as they appeared. All he wants is to get home and forward seems to be the right direction, the only direction.

Since the sycamore accident Chenko finds himself in the first set of adverse circumstances he's had to face. Given everything that has happened so far, it is the first situation to present challenges. There's no visibility and it's getting cold. It's unexpected, uncomfortable and Chenko wonders how long it will last. The light and warmth he was starting to take for granted is now absent. The change in environment takes him by surprise. He'll find the unpredictable also exists in this dimension.

Maybe two to three hundred feet down the road the light of a small fire comes in view. Its right in front of him, he doesn't have to turn his head, but the tapping branch takes him to the left of the fire, there's a bend in the road, he thinks. The road is not a straight line to the fire like he first thought. As he weaves his way in total darkness the fire becomes clearer as he slowly feels his way forward, tapping out his arrival in some unknown code.

The smells of canvas, diesel and gunpowder fill the air. The smells and the sound of the hard surface he taps the only company he has as hemoves toward the fire, unsure if this is a good idea. But all he can see in the distance is the fire, nothing more, and all he can feel is the cold, which make it seem like a good idea. Thinking he made his choice and he'll take his chances.

When Chenko enters the light of the fire, he notices he's now wearing an olive drab tee-shirt, the big pocket pants of jungle fatigues, canvas boots with one of his two dog tags laced to the right boot and the other hanging from a chain around his neck. He also appears to be the age of when he wore jungle fatigues in the Army.

By the fire a man, the same age as Chenko appears, is dressed in worn out camouflage fatigues, he's barefoot and appears tired. He pokes a stick into the fire and asks "Whose army are you in?" The man had seen Russians and Americans.

For a moment the question brings Chenko back to the time when he was in the Army. Precisely what he sees is the time he was pulled from the field and sent home. The way he showed up to the transfer point caused some Major to ask the same question, as Chenko stood before him with no name tag, rank or any other form of identification visible on his uniform. He remembers he looked at his dog tag and then answered the Major, "Last time I checked, the United States Army. Why? Has there been a change? Sir." The recollection made him feel what he really wanted to tell the Major "Does it matter?" which is what he tells the man by the fire.

The man answers "Guess not, I can't kill you now." Like Chenko, aware of all the changes from how his day started out and him now sitting by the fire he built deep in the woods, hiding out. What he says reveals the thought is still there, but the possibility doesn't exist in this dimension. Both intuitively know this now, so there's no point in getting into it. Chenko answers "Never saw much point in killing who you don't know."

What the man thought was deep in the woods, was close to a road, he has no idea there is a road two hundred to three hundred feet in front of him and winds within fifty feet of his fire. Had he known he would have gotten farther from it to build his fire, he knows roads are targets.

He's no stranger to the ambushes that take place on them. It's not until he hears Chenko's tapping that he becomes aware. At first it sounded like code to him, coming from one direction and then another, always getting closer. It's not until he sees the branch in Chenko's hand in the light of the fire that it comes to him. Chenko was like some blind person stepping into the light of his fire.

His name is Andwar; he's from the Middle East, was with either the Hezbollah or Hamas or Taliban or Fatah, or any of the others, but he wasn't in an army, he was in a militia that fought armies.

He was working a rocket launcher when fate sighted him and he got vaporized in an artillery barrage. From a rival militia that got sidetracked from the fight and took the opportunity to settle some old score, several centuries old, that no one could really remember other than it still existed.

It was an ironic twist of fate that he was in a militia that was different from the tribe of the militia that had the big guns and still unwilling to forget. For a moment he became a better target than the infidels both militias were engaging and their supposed prime objective. The bad blood between the two militias is always there and he became a target of opportunity. Andwar has figured out he wasn't killed by any infidel. Like Chenko his end isn't what he expected.

The difference between Chenko and Andwar, in their other lives, is Chenko was in an army for no more than two years; Andwar was in a militia for nine years, ever since he was sixteen. Chenko offers Andwar a cigarette. The cigarettes

Chenko pulls from his deep pockets surprises him, but is what he smoked at the time.

Andwar is apprehensive in taking it, it's not good for him, not good for anyone, but yet at the same time it is enticing. Andwar is no stranger to tobacco and a whole host of other vices he's not supposed to have, but has. It's what he and Chenko find they have in common as they talk and recall their human side in another life. The real conflict they faced in life, their free will versus the will of God. Told them by clergy and clerics yet to experience the dimension they're in.

Another difference is that Chenko was in a war and survived, Andwar was killed in a war, but it's a small difference when compared to the fact both were soldiers, this is their common ground. Both are at the same place in the end and how each got there is secondary to this shared experience, their conviction, their involvement, their apathy.

The convictions to their cause, their involvement in trying enforce their cause and their apathy of any flaw in their cause. Both know all three are part of a process that in the end defies common sense, but each step became something they did with little or no questioning. The lives that have to be taken, the maimed, refugees, destroyed terrain; all take a back seat to the cause. In the world of logic all counter-productive to what should be. Both talk about this now.

There are no seventy-two virgins for Andwar and Chenko is yet to meet Christ. It doesn't seem to be the way they were once told. Both still hold to their faith in this dimension, it's an option in this dimension. Intuitively they know now it is what will get them out of this dimension, but it can't be blind.

Each now aware their faith has not left them, even though nothing has turned out as they expect. In one way or the other, both understand now it was their blind faith in some of the causes they took up in another life that put them in front of the fire they now share in another dimension. Both are aware of this now.

The light of the fire and the warmth it provides is maintained as they talk, Chenko gathers broken branches and Andwar feeds the fire. They talk of rashes and stings they got from being in the same type of terrain in another life, the diarrhea and fevers they picked up carrying the fight to the enemy. The enemy now a minor subject to the misery brought on by these events of discomfort in addition to the violence. They begin to joke about conditions they found themselves in, in another life, in a gross and humorous way only two soldiers are capable of, noticing all the unpleasant side effects of that time are now gone by the fire they share.

Andwar tells Chenko he can't remember the last time he ate. He continues that it's strange because he feels no hunger, but yet at the same time could eat. It's more a desire than a necessity. Chenko understands what he's saying. There is no hunger in this dimension, but there is appetite. Chenko tells Andwar of the kitchen he came from before running into his fire.

He tells him about the coffee, food, and service, when the sun comes up, they'll go there. Chenko decides at that moment he won't tell Andwar how to get there, but instead will take him there, even though he'll be going backwards instead of forward.

It's not too long after they make their plans both find a place to sleep within the light and warmth of their fire. Their slumber is unlike any sleep they have ever known. When the morning comes, they begin the journey and it's not long before the trees become full and grasses and wild flowers flourish on the roadside and both joke about how the other is now dressed.

Chenko sits on the corner of the bed still waiting for Ilene. "I'm walking towards you, always. When I come into view, you'll see me as I am, not as I was. Have a coin in my pocket for you. But seems you'll have to wait."

******

Chenko leaves Andwar at the kitchen; they both know they'll see each other again. Both have now made a friend in this dimension, this is important. Chenko walks a road now that is wide and made of concrete. Cars and trucks of all sizes and colors are in continuous motion, moving in both directions, some are old, others new, some look to be in good shape and others don't. Same with the people he passes.

The road goes by a river running through the industrial part of a town; on the banks of the river are railroad tracks, on the tracks are boxcars and coal cars in front of warehouses and factories.

There are bridges, tunnels and alleys leading to neighborhoods of old houses. The buildings and houses stand in defiance of time. Time wants them gone and that's what has happened to them, they are "time's" victims, all the buildings and houses that were torn, blown, or burned down the day Chenko hit the sycamore. They're all property that once was and now is no more; all having found their way to this dimension.

Most are obsolete, made this way by buildings and houses in other towns, in other states or countries that became more efficient in manufacturing than what these buildings and houses provided. There are newer buildings and houses that met their fate by being in front of a tornado or bad wiring, but they're the exception not the rule. The buildings and houses are like the souls that share this dimension. In short, there are many ways to this dimension, too many to mention, for the souls and structures.

Chenko stops on a bridge; he's halfway across it when he pauses to light a cigar and looks at all that surrounds him. It's a fine smoke and has to be enjoyed by being stationary and becoming a visionary. The river flows under the bridge, the water isn't clear, but it's the same dark blue color everywhere on the surface, there are no oil slicks or debris, it's free of what doesn't belong on it or in it. It seems to look and flow like it did before the factory and houses showed up. The buildings, houses are no longer adversaries to the river, all are now in balance.

Up from the river bank and by the tracks are large asphalt parking lots where plants randomly fight through the cracks in their surface for their lives, trees are scarce. The colors of the sparse plants and trees are in contrast to the red brick, grey cinder block and silver windows. The plants and trees down here are like the people who made the area their home in another life, tough and strong willed. Displayed on some of the box cars by these lots the graffiti from some of the places they've been. Some of the designs are well done, others aren't, some designs are pleasing, and other designs are disturbing.

The smoke pours from Chenko's nose and mouth as he leans on the rail overlooking everything and he becomes aware he's the only one around, there is not a soul in sight. Yet he notices windows that were closed on first glance are now open when glanced at again. Coal and boxcars that were in front of some of the buildings are now gone, revealing large doors that just took in what they delivered. The freight on some docks has been moved, docks that were empty are now full of freight. With every second glance Chenko notices everything that has changed from his first glance. There's constant movement, but he can't see it. He's alone, but he isn't alone.

It doesn't bother him. With each hit from his smoke, he becomes lost in another life when he was in the same type of environment, only back then it seemed more uncomfortable. He starts to look at the ground and his eyes wander its surface for the cigarette butts, empty bottles, old tires, discarded appliances and trash that are now absent. In another life this part of town was full of debris, everything was thrown to ground the moment after it was consumed, including the people.

There's nothing on the ground. The streets are clean. Those who he can't see, but he knows are around, must now be different and seem to have overcome the debris of another life. It's not that the buildings and houses in the area aren't without their scars; it's that they now wear them in a better light.

All the injuries and diseases found in another life in this part of town, here seem to be healing. There are still plenty of things that need to be fixed and there's a feeling the repairs are coming. There is a feeling the area is becoming what it should be instead of what it once was. All the movement Chenko feels tells him this.

It's a strange and good feeling Chenko has on the bridge. Chenko has no idea what seems to make it work now, other than some form of hope coming to life. All he knows is how this area use to be and how it became that way. In another life when men starting making things, the most efficient way to get rid of what they couldn't use was the river. It wasn't right, but the fact it was efficient made it right. A system where a few benefitted at the expense of many became acceptable at the time in a place like this. In another life what was practiced in this part of town was taking advantage of one another.

Chenko makes his way off the bridge and walks past the front of a factory. It's made of dark brick and when it was built had a lot of masons working the scaffolds. All the windows and doors trimmed in a uniform pattern accenting their location. Five steps, that run a length of fifty or so feet, lead up to the entrance that is under a large stone arch, the keystone has Roman numerals carved in it. The building is the result of good management and skilled labor, its appearance one of strength and capability.

The factory building takes up a block, at every corner across the street on every side are the small shops and businesses. When Chenko comes to a corner, the diners and taverns, corner grocery stores and movie theaters, to his left hold his interest and instead of going straight he turns in their direction. He thinks to himself it's like going through an industrial forest, the factory like the sycamore surrounded by its children.

Still not a soul in sight, but as Chenko moves on he can sense their presence, can feel their movement, he just can't see those who occupy what he is passing through. But he can feel the balance they have with all that surrounds them, which he can see. He sees where they live and work, but can't see them. It's unlike any feeling he had in another life. "What makes it work?" He wonders and this is the feeling he has about those who he knows surround him; everything works the way it should for these unseen souls now. All he can process is a sensation it's well deserved and the unseen souls earned it from another life.

Seems he remembers in another life the part of town he's now enjoying was the part of town everyone wanted to get out of. The souls in this part of town were hard pressed. If you were from this neighborhood everyone knew it. It didn't take much to notice those who live hand to mouth and nothing more. It was the part of town that was hard to escape. If you did get out, this part of town went with you, it's never forgotten. It's the part of town where taverns turn into saloons, there's gambling at the corner grocery, and the theaters are replaced by strip joints. It's the part of town filled with all kinds of debris. In this part of town there's little or no balance. This what Chenko recalls from another life. What he sees and feels now is totally different.

All the recollections of this part of town were recollections of conflict. In the beginning, those who owned what was in this part of town were more prone to take advantage of those who worked and lived there. The owners have a long history; most of it is good, but not all of it. For example, the time they tried to pull the "company scrip" that was only good at the "company store," where the necessities sold were priced just beyond the wages paid. Putting the worker always in debt, but more important than this, totally dependent, their labor frozen in one place for one owner. Most know this isn't right, but there are a few who think it is. They're usually the ones who own the company and the store. For a while the owners pulled it off until it was stopped after a lot of skull-busting.

In the beginning it was a stacked deck for those who sold their labor, the owners had influence with those who made the laws. Didn't take much to get some boys from the law to come down on any place labor was acting up. But they didn't go away, after a while they made it so every time the law did show up things got worse instead of better. After a while each conflict only strengthened their organization. Eventually the workers got some of their boys voted in and the laws changed to the way it should be.

One would think a balance had been reached and call it human nature, but then organized labor gets in bed with the organized crime. They tried to pull off the "ghost" employee, charging for work that is never done, it's as bad as the company store, between the two, one is always trying to take advantage of the other, always in conflict instead of balance.

Chenko thinks this is the part of town you'd find the company stores and the ghost employees in another life. He feels some relief being where he is now, the balance that was missing in this part of town in another life feels like its present now and unexplainable.

It's beyond all he ever heard about Adam Smith, the rise of capitalism and the "invisible hand." It's beyond Karl Marx and the rise of socialisms "from each according to his abilities, to each according to his need." The division of labor, of who does what and who gets what, that has plagued man from the beginning of time Chenko concludes doesn't matter where he stands now.

If he had to explain where he stands now, it would be the unseen around him have found a bride in one system and a groom in the other and made a marriage to their benefit. It's all processed by Chenko in the clarity of his new language and beyond the words we have to explain it.

He moves deeper into this part of town, sidetracked by what he sees and feels. Chenko is becoming lost; he's no longer going forward. He smells food cooking as he walks past the diners; it smells good, red lights turn yellow and then green; the neon lights are on in the tavern windows. Glances change from moment to moment, but not only can he not see those around him, he cannot hear them, all he can hear is movement, a plate crashing to a floor in a diner he passes, the ring of a cash register by an open tavern door.

All he hears are the sounds of activity with no visibility of who produces them. A feeling comes that those who are around him were as unseen in another life as they are to him now. He can't leave this part of town until he sees and hears them to make up for this.

In a way he feels trapped. Hearing and seeing them now becomes like a requirement. He has to gain the vision he once ignored before he can move on. Chenko moves past the shops, stores and theatres, stopping in front of a bakery.

Before him is every type of cake, pie and pastry. He decides to go in, but is stopped by a reflection in the window, its M T sitting on a bench behind him. M T has his legs crossed and is working a deck of cards, he smiles and signals Chenko to come sit with him. The faint translucent shapes of people begin to appear around M T, all going about their business. They can barely be seen and their conversations barely heard, but they are beginning to surface.

Chenko remains with his back to M T feeling as soon as he turns around M T and the images of the others will be gone and tells him "No you come here." He is beginning to stand his ground in this dimension. M T laughs and answers "Fine." Immediately appearing next to him and begins to look at what Chenko is looking at, saying nothing more.

As they look at the window Chenko moves around M T acting like he wants a different view, but using the opportunity to nudge M T so he can feel him, to see if he is real. M T takes notice and laughs even more, "You have no idea how real I am," knowing exactly what Chenko is doing. It catches Chenko off guard and he breaks contact immediately, feeling instead of hearing M T, experiencing both pleasure and pain at the same time from the contact, it scares Chenko.

"Who are you?" Chenko begins. M T answers "I own that question and it's not for sale. You don't want to ask me... It's a question you should ask yourself." Chenko is unimpressed with M T's answer, in another life it sounded like something from a motivational tape or seminar. He answers M T "I know who I am. You're the question mark here." Trying to corner M T.

There is something about M T Chenko likes, he has a nice edge to him and Chenko knows he doesn't want feel how sharp it is, and begins to back off his true nature, which is beginning to surface. He senses who would win a war of wills between them.

M T has an appearance Chenko respects, in build and dress. His tee shirt carrying the design of the crop circle provides a clue that can't be overlooked, that M T knows more about Chenko than maybe Chenko knows about himself. Chenko reaches a decision; he has no reason not to trust him. He tells M T in a respectful voice "You're Emmett, two 'm's', two 't's' Got it." M T gives a nonchalant nod. "All you need to process for right now."

As they look at the baked goods in the window M T tells Chenko "The food of celebrations, birthdays, receptions, the holidays and evening snacks, even death days." A discussion commences between them, Chenko thinking in another life there were lot of pounds in the window, after a while one never got to eat their fill in fear of the weight they would gain.

M T tells Chenko. "I know, Mass in the universe is constant, if someone is losing weight, someone is gaining it." It's exactly what Chenko is going to say next and for a moment GM and the Anzio prayer flash through his mind. Only Chenko is like GM this time. M T's tee-shirt is not lost on Chenko and Chenko begins to notice M T is starting to speak in appearance as well as words.

M T tells Chenko that type of weight isn't a factor anymore, where Chenko now exists, from here on out what he eats and how much won't add a pound, neither will a pound be lost if he chose not to eat. The only weight that matters here is the weight of spirit and flesh. One is a good weight; one is a bad weight; one better outweigh the other.

M T tells Chenko eventually he'll run into a set of scales waiting for him down the road, a set of scales waits for everyone. There's a good and bad eternity determined by the weight of spirit and flesh.

What M T tells Chenko is nothing new; the concept was a big part of another life, but in this dimension Chenko becomes totally aware of how important it is now, now it is real.

He begins to process all M T is telling him and it becomes clear the only weight that can be gained and lost is reserved for spirit and flesh in this dimension and the weight doesn't come from food. Here some gain weight in spirit others in flesh, it all comes down now to the choices made about what weight to put on or take off in the good and bad situations one will find themselves in this dimension, as Chenko is to find out in greater detail.

******

M T walks into the bakery, Chenko is unable to move, stuck in the position he assumed after making contact with M T. All he can do is watch and for the first time sees another person, not an image, put a dozen maple cream sticks in a box and pour two cups of coffee. The man in the shop, like the driver who picked up M T, is someone Chenko knows, but can't place.

They head to the park bench M T first appeared on and begin to work on the sticks and cups. Chenko asks about the guy in the shop, M T ignores the questions, telling Chenko he has something he wants Chenko to give someone. It's a mission.

M T begins to tell of the time Chenko had the "usual" that Jazz brought to him and how he searched for someone he knew. Next M T produces a small package, wrapped in brown paper, bound by white string about the size of a pack of cigarettes and gives it to Chenko.

M T points to a tavern down the street. "There's someone in there you know. When you see him, give him this." M T tells Chenko, it's his choice to do this. It's something Chenko doesn't have to do right away or at all, that he should think about it for a while. Chenko begins to process what he's being told, there's an implied risk in this mission that is in perfect balance with its importance to M T.

Before M T leaves Chenko, he takes an inventory of all Chenko has received since entering the dimension both share now, he asks about the coin Chenko has in his pocket when he thought it was empty and Chenko places his hand in his pants pocket and rubs it. Then he asks about the two of hearts and Chenko pulls it from his shirt pocket. Chenko accepts the small package from M T. The small package goes into the pocket with the coin.

The mission is on. M T tells Chenko he now has three items, two that are to be kept always and one that is to be given away, don't make the mistake of giving away what is to be kept and keeping what is to be given away. Where he's sending Chenko that could happen. M T leaves Chenko with one last thought. "Any wound you receive here will not heal; any wound you give another here will not be forgotten."

This time M T walks off and disappears in the horizon. Chenko watches from the bench trying to reach some decision on the package. M T's last words a riddle filled with caution and no mention of reward. Chenko sits on the bed still waiting for Ilene. He subconsciously reaches for a cigar, but he's out, muttering to himself. "Just as well." He's still working on what to say to her. "I'm walking towards you, always. When I come into view, you'll see me as I am, not as I was. I have a coin in my pocket for you. It seems you'll have to wait. I'm just as confused as you are."

******

Taking M T's advice Chenko takes his time processing what he will do next. He's caught between two places, the kitchen he now returns to often and the part of town that has the tavern where he's been told he knows someone. It will be this way for as long as he has the package, he accepted from M T. He talks to Jazz and Andwar and shows them the package, tells them about M T, seeking their advice.

What the three of them do now is very similar to what they did in another life. The situation Chenko tells them he's in results in both asking more questions than giving answers. Each easily sidetracked, telling the other about their situation. They share what they have with each other in trying to solve the other's problems. Problems are also part of this dimension, their sharing; part of the process leading to release from this dimension.

Andwar has a cave to visit, only he doesn't have to give anyone anything, he has a diary he has to retrieve. It's written in his hand and has many pages; he knows there is one page that will determine his outcome; this is what he's been told. Jazz is still working her mirror waiting for her mom. Andwar knows about the diary, but has no idea where the cave is. Jazz's compact has become like a cell phone in another life, she puts it down here and there, then spends time looking for it in a panic that her mom will show up when she can't find it. When she misplaces it all look for the compact.

Andwar spends his time drinking endless cups of coffee and becoming a radio head, tuning in to all the conversations around him in search of clues. The head set is always on.

One evening he hears the conversation two tables away, between four or maybe five men, about some rocket launching fool who got in their sights and a diary they found after taking over some position. After reading it they left it in some cave. They were all shot down by Andwar's militia leaving the cave a few hours after he was killed.

They also are interested in finding the diary. Andwar is in a race with them. They were there one night and Andwar is yet to see them again. Like Chenko in his bedroom, Andwar is wandering some unknown province looking for a cave as he drinks coffee.

Jazz has a friend named Rita. Just like Chenko described the vanity to Jazz, Rita has described Jazz's mom to her on a number of occasions, telling Jazz "She's been in more than once." Jazz has even given Rita her compact, but her mom's reflection can only be seen by Jazz, she has to have it in her hand, the hand of another won't work. There's hope in what Rita tells Jazz and there is a feeling her mom's memories and dreams of Jazz are getting stronger. Jazz and Rita are never far from each other working the tables waiting for the moment to arrive. Jazz is working the tables while at the same time sitting in some hospital trying to get her on mom on the phone.

Chenko, Jazz and Andwar go back and forth on all they face. Each has their own M T. Each wait for them to appear as they eat, drink and smoke, wondering what to do after the encounters, taking and ignoring suggestions like they did in another life. The three find comfort in each other and each is able to help lessen their apprehensions of what to do next.

******

One day a signal comes from Jazz to Rita, a reflection is caught. She held on and her mother wouldn't let go, the reflection of their love will stay. Jazz is gone. She makes weight.

One night the band of men return and Andwar picks up he's searching the wrong province, learns the right one and finds what he's after. Evening the score, leaving the men two tables down to continue an endless search for what is no longer there.

Chenko is alone. Any thought of missing them is replaced by the joy of Jazz and Andwar achieving what he has yet to achieve. It's soon after the day of reflection and night of the diary that Chenko sets out for the tavern.

Next morning as he finishes his first cup of coffee without their company, he's struck with the knowledge it will be his last in this place. Chenko looks around and there are fewer vacant stares and threatening gestures and more smiles. He'd been to the kitchen a lot and it seemed to him he was getting used to everyone and they were getting used to him. The food and drink were great, so were the smokes, he made some friends here. Just as he was finding some comfort he has to leave and a sentimental feeling comes over him, beyond any he felt in another life. It's become a hard place to leave and takes most of the day.

M T stands under a street light, leaning on it, smoking, as Chenko says his good byes and finally finds the door. Once outside, the first thing Chenko sees is M T in his circle of light. At first, he can't make M T out, but within five steps he knows who is in the light. Chenko smiles. "You again, how's it going?" M T smiles back. "Who'd you expect? Where you going?" Chenko returns only a partial smile unable to mask some concern. "You know where I'm going." M T nods and says "Remember all I told you." There's no smile. M T hesitates, and then continues... "Wait, before you head out, I want to show you something."

The two smoke their ash less, disappearing cigars as they walk and make small talk of sports, women, food and other subjects from another life. They laugh and joke about them. It's a pleasant walk and an interesting conversation. When they're finished and the cigars disappear, they're standing in the warehouse district of a town. There are big and small warehouses, some are brick others wood, some are in good shape, others aren't.

M T and Chenko wander between and around them, M T acting like he's looking for one in particular, but knows exactly where he's going. He stops and looks up at the name over the doors of what Chenko can see is a big warehouse, it's not the biggest around, but it's big. When Chenko looks up at what M T is looking at he sees his name "Ananias Ezra Zachenko." As M T unlocks the door, he asks Chenko "Ever wonder how much toilet paper you used in another life?"

It's another sycamore experience for Chenko as M T leads him around the warehouse. The answer to his question is found in a huge room he shows Chenko filled from floor to ceiling with every sheet of toilet paper he used; only now back in its original roll, taking up an immense amount of floor space. M T continues… "A lot of food behind that paper. Here let me show you." Chenko is shown the area holding every single bite of food he'd taken from steaks to C-rations, from parfaits to popsicles, he consumed back in their original state, stacked floor to ceiling. Meat and potatoes with every kind of food in between. Every toothpick, tube of toothpaste, anything he consumed in life, including gasoline, hair tonic, medicine, band aids, tires, it was all there, everything, back to its original state, to give Chenko some idea of the dimension of his consumption. Chenko is beyond amazement.

M T goes to one of the many clipboards hanging-on the concrete support posts, reads off a number to Chenko of how many paper napkins he used wiping his mouth and waits for him to speak. All Chenko can do is shake his head, still lost in the size of the number. A space of time passes and M T continues "It's all here from napkins to tissues." M T continues "Now, most of this you earned. But some of it you stole. You stole when you ate more food than you should have and used more fuel than you needed, when you wasted what could have gone to others...What you stole is in a part of this warehouse, I won't show you now, but maybe later. Everyone is a thief."

One unfortunate fact can't be overlooked as Chenko processes all M T shows and tells him. On more than one occasion he was guilty of theft. He's seen most of the warehouse, but not all of it and tries to figure what portion he hasn't been shown. He's unable to get a clear idea of how big the area of what he stole would be, but he doesn't doubt it's there. The only clarity he can find is that the area is now a concern, and probably adds bad weight. He thinks to himself what if the area is bigger than one of the smaller neighboring warehouses? M T reads Chenko's mind and comments as he locks up "You've got the biggest house on the block." It concerns Chenko.

They walk towards the bridge and stop in the middle and have a smoke before parting. Chenko thinks of one of the comments M T made on the bench in front of the bakery. "Next time, down here things will be different, those you couldn't see in another life you'll see now." Chenko doesn't need to ask what M T meant, it's answered by M T the moment the thought comes to his mind. "Those you helped and those you hurt without knowing...In the end they're the ones who decide."

M T tells Chenko the small package Chenko has in his pocket is for someone who's been running from him. He tells Chenko not only does Chenko know this person, Chenko knows the person who is sending the package, it's not him, but someone M T knows and this person chose Chenko to make the delivery. The person sending it is someone they both know, the person receiving it is someone now only Chenko knows. All M T is doing is setting it up; he's the go-between. M T ignores all questions Chenko has about the persons involved. Finally, Chenko realizes M T is good at ignoring his questions and realizes he has to answer the questions he has about them himself.

M T tells Chenko he's no longer going to chase this guy and Chenko is really doing the guy a favor by accepting the mission to deliver the package from the guy they both know. By doing so Chenko is this guy's last chance to come clean with M T. "Tell him he can't hide it. Tell him I want it back." M T instructs Chenko.

He tells Chenko he's sending him to a part of town where all around him will know how much he helped or hurt them. M T ends, "Now they can help or hurt you. They're the difference between easy and hard in what you have to do. Remember don't give away what is to be kept and don't keep what is to be given away." M T, for the first time, disappears in front of Chenko, punctuating the situation.

Chenko walks past the dark brick factory and beyond the bakery. He's surrounded by people he can see and hear. He can't help but notice they move with purpose and there's a harmony in what they are doing. They move in and out of the buildings and homes engaged in some productive activity. Mostly they unload, transport and warehouse what other souls consumed in another life.

Some work in the factories supplying the parts and materials to keep everything moving. It's an economy built on death. They'd do more, but seem to be plagued by shortages. They repair what needs repairing with what they have and tend to small gardens, sweep the streets and talk and joke with each other about the warehouses on the hill that overlook them and all they hold that they could use. They smile and nod at Chenko and say little as he passes by.

Two blocks away Chenko sees the pink and blue neon lights of the Slip Away Tavern. The light bounces around the atmosphere and colors the sky like the Aurora Borealis. The Slip Away will become just as big a mystery. It's inviting and mystical. As Chenko gets closer he notices most walk by the tavern, few go in and no one has come out. He stops and has a cigar and watches for someone to come out, before he goes in.

The cigar disappears and no one has come out, this concerns Chenko and he becomes apprehensive about going in and wishes Jazz and Andwar were with him. He stops a passer-by. "Excuse me, you ever been in the Slip Away?" The man answers with a stare. "Just once. More go in than come out." He returns to the smile he wore before the question, says nothing more, and moves on.

The way he looked and the way he answered the question, were far from an endorsement to go in. The smile the man gave in the end seemed to come from the knowledge he didn't need to do it again. But he gives Chenko enough of an answer to make a decision. The guy did go in and the guy did come out, it's enough to make Chenko take his first deep breath in this dimension and go in. He doesn't want to keep the package.

On the outside the Slip Away looks small, but once inside it's the biggest tavern, bar or saloon Chenko has ever been in. In fact, it's like every bar Chenko has ever been in, in another life, from fine expensive woodwork to sandbags. Every type, neighborhood, sports, pickup, strip, are in sections to be wandered through, each section with its own unique personality. It's crowded and has the good and bad atmosphere of an endless Saint Patrick's Day and everyone is from someplace like Wisconsin. Chenko, so far, is comfortable with it.

Chenko feels a slap on his back, he turns to see who gave it; thinking it might be the person he's looking for. It turns out to be no one he knows, but the stranger is offering to get him a drink, "I can see you are way behind." Chenko accepts and the man tells him how he gave the bartender the card given when he showed up in this dimension. "First thing they got," when he came into the place looking for someone. "They'll ask for it, found out too late you don't have to give it to them. All the drinks are on the house. They don't have to tell 'ya. They'll con ya." He can't tell Chenko how long he's been at the Slip Away or how many drinks he's had. He confesses "Been here so long I don't know who I'm looking for anymore...Could be you!"

It's not hard to pick up the man is becoming agitated the more he talks about his situation and who he's looking for, willing to accept Chenko as the one he's looking for even though he knows he's wrong. He just wants it to be over so he can get out. Aside from his growing agitation that this might not happen, Chenko is actually fortunate to run into him, he's giving Chenko a lot of information that will help. Information he didn't have to give or maybe didn't want to give, but had pounded down enough drinks to let Chenko see what can happen in the Slip Away. Whether the man knew it or not, he helped Chenko.

A thirty-two ounce clear glass mug is put in front of Chenko, ordered by the man who gave up his card. The liquid held in the mug is in three colors, the bottom third is clear, the middle third is golden, and the top third is red. No matter how one tips or twirls the clear glass mug the liquids keep their integrity and don't mix together. It's puzzling. The first third is like fine wine, the second, top shelf blended whiskey. The bottom third is the surprise; it's like the best heavy duty pharmaceuticals in pure liquid form. When they get inside a person, they mix with each other fueling perceptions at an unsafe speed where everything becomes unclear and unpredictable.

It doesn't take Chenko long to throw it down and understand what the man is telling him about losing sight of what has to be done. It's the most powerful drink he's ever had. But to Chenko's credit he still holds on to what the drink cost the man and to what M T told him about what to keep and what to give away. The knowledge floats on the surface of the mixture now inside him, like a small boat in uncertain seas, taking on water.

He thanks the man, but doesn't return the favor. The man is okay with this, he knows he's past some point of no return. He warns Chenko. "Don't give up your card...Don't give up anything." He asks Chenko. "You sure you're not missing a pen? I've got a pen I gotta give somebody."

All Chenko wants to do is break away from him and work with the heavy buzz he feels coming on. He shakes hands with the stranger and thanks him more than once, then makes his move. As he wanders off he's struck for a moment and he sees his barn, the company he kept one afternoon, the dream he had and the oracles he saw, wondering if this is a dream. He's unsure what is happening.

Chenko wanders from one section to another, having never been so loaded and still on his feet. He hears amazing conversations on politics and sex, but none on religion, it's replaced by sports. The atmosphere is fascinating, a million thoughts crowd his mind from all he hears and sees. The ability to process is still fast, but not as clear, airbrushed. He doesn't care. He's no longer looking for anyone; he's looking at everyone.

Everyone and everything are fascinating, including him. The mixture within telling him there isn't anything he can't do and this is the place to let everyone know. The audience for everything he ever wanted to do is now in front of him and he's ready to perform.

All the things he ever wanted to do he feels he can do now, such as walking up on the stage and telling the lead singer to move over and the lead guitar to surrender all six strings. Saddling up and telling the boys to follow him, grabbing the mike, breaking into the perfect rendition of Fred Eaglesmith's *Alcohol and Pills,* sounding great and looking buff in the perfect tee-shirt and jeans, on stage barefoot making all the right moves. All the good-looking chicks are digging him, pulling up their tops and throwing their panties on the stage. There's little resentment from the boys, he becomes the male yardstick and speaks for all of them.

Chenko does exactly this in one section and spends a lot of time looking for what he shouldn't be looking for and finding this out the hard way. He's well received on and off the stage, but the longer he stays, the more his audience wants, but it's never enough and it begins to agitate him and he begins to agitate them.

There something about receiving all the benefits of the flesh with no commitment given in return, that doesn't feel right. Moving on from one song to another and one chick to another, everything is so temporary, there's no satisfaction. If there is any spirit behind what he does in this section of the Slip Away, it's the wrong spirit. He can change the feeling he has by stopping what he's doing; then again, he could refuel and get another drink and keep trying to smooth his and their attitudes.

Chenko chooses the drink, at this point he doesn't care what it costs, the mixture in him telling him everything is fine and will get better if he keeps topping off the tank. He has a card, a coin in his pocket, a package; he's rich; so, whatever it takes to get what he wants. Doesn't matter anymore what he's to keep and give away. All his perceptions are now blurred. He starts making his way to the bar. Forgetting what he's been told, that everything is on the house. He doesn't have to give up anything. It's a big mistake.

But fate steps in, just like it did in another life and halfway to a bartender eagerly waiting to take advantage of him or anyone else in the place, he's stopped by a voice coming from a dark section he passes through. "Hey college boy!" Chenko recognizes the voice; it's the first voice he's heard in this dimension from another life, it's Gandy's voice. What could be better!?

But when he turns towards the voice, he sees the darkest of the all the villains he's ever known – Lump. It's a shock and the feeling of being tricked by a friendly voice to this outcome is sobering. It's the first time it's happened in this dimension, but it's the mixture inside of him that lets him hear one thing and see another that tricks him.

There Lump sits. Looking like every villain portrayed on screen and literature wrapped up in to one ultimate villain. His eyes let you know he's not beyond blackjacks, brass knuckles, knives and guns, that he exists to inflict slow and painful outcomes to those he feels have cheated him, which is everyone.

The only purpose he has is to get the drop on whoever crosses his path and go to work, always driven by the philosophy that's what the other person would do, having lost faith in human nature long ago. Those who cross his path deserve what they get. A villain who has no problem excusing what he does. He's always felt he's been the victim and because of this he has no remorse. This is what Chenko sees in his eyes.

For a moment Chenko wants to see M T and tell him off. He's upset. But he's unaware of what is really happening, later on M T will point out to Chenko, he never found Lump, Lump found him. It's a technicality M T will always bring up to tease Chenko when Chenko tells him of the delivery he made for M T. M T will also tell him he didn't make the delivery for him, but for someone else, another technicality.

Chenko starts out. "You haven't changed a bit." There's no smile when he says it. Lump smiles not in friendship, but in desire to go to work. "Sit down. I'll get you a drink." For a moment Chenko sees the pop machine in Gandy's shop and knows what to do. He waves off the offer, but does sit down. He's struck by the irony of the drink he started out for, that he really wanted, and how it's so easily refused now. Knowing it's the last thing he needs. What he needs is to go to work and get the package delivered and get out. Clarity returns to all he is processing, nothing is airbrushed now, all the scars are visible.

Lump is the first person in this dimension to have an odor about him, and Chenko can smell the stale smoke, cheap whiskey and drugs from another life coming from him. Lump sits with a white handkerchief that is becoming pink and dark red from the blood coming from a gash over his left eye, continually dabbing it in the gash. Over in one corner is a pile of dark red handkerchiefs that can't absorb any more blood. He can't get it to stop bleeding, the reason he sits in a dark corner, so no one can see his wound and take advantage of him.

Chenko sees his false teeth wrapped in the same filthy handkerchief on the table. Somewhere along the line he caught a huge right hand. He tells Chenko about the fight he got into when he first came into the Slip Away as if Chenko were some long lost buddy from the old days interested in its brutal outcome. Happy Lump won; something not to be forgotten. What Lump recalls about those days is totally different from what Chenko recalls all the fights he'd seen Lump in back then. One thing for sure, there's no doubt in Chenko's mind who started the fight and put him in this dark corner, there's no doubt in his mind that the gash over his left eye is well deserved.

Lump goes on to tell Chenko he ducked into the place to get away from some other guy looking for him. Tells him of the painful heart attack he had in his driveway. Tried to flag down some guy who blew by on a Sportster who didn't see him, last thing he saw before running into this guy... "We don't get along at all." This doesn't come as any surprise to Chenko.

The whole time pretending Chenko and he are long lost friends and Chenko cares. Needing a friend, but knowing it's too late. Chenko doesn't care or pretend. "I know. The guy wants you to have this." He throws the package on the table. "Wants you to know you can't hide it." Chenko lights a smoke and gets ready for anything.

When the package hit the table, technically the mission ended successfully and Chenko is free to leave, but he stays to see what the package holds. Lump unties the string, removes the brown paper and un-wraps the bubble wrap. When he comes to what the package holds, he drops it immediately on the table no different than if it were some hot embers that fate put in his hands. He's scorched by what he feels and sees. It's painful.

A bright, silver eight slash Zippo Storm King lighter bounces once on the table and comes to a rest on the side where the letter "D" is visible. It's a crude rendering, far from professional, but its carved deep into the lighter's surface and can't be missed. It's Donnie's, Chenko recognizes it right away. Donnie never smoked, but loved lighting other people's smokes. It was the one thing he carried that made him like the rest of the guys. Chenko would know it anywhere and whispers to himself "Donnie and his lighter Mr. Fisher a light please."

Chenko looks at Lump and Lump begins to tell Chenko of how he ran into Donnie one night in a town he was passing through. The dark corner begins to take on the appearance of an interview room at some police station where the confrontation is over and the confession begins. Lump confessing that Donnie was the last guy he expected to run into and when he did it didn't take long to figure out Donnie had a gas station and was doing a lot better than him. It didn't seem right to Lump. "What's *he* doing with a gas station!?"

He robbed Donnie, worked him over pretty good with his brass knuckles. He didn't expect Donnie to die, but he did. Left Donnie in a heap inside the station, his wife and kids found him the next morning.

Took his lighter, never got caught. Lump makes his excuse, "If I hadn't been totally loaded at the time, maybe things would've turned out different. Sure, didn't mean for it to happen. It was an accident." As if this clears everything up, as if he was the victim in this accident. Lump never tells Chenko he cut off Donnie's left hand to get the wedding band. It's too much for him to share.

All Chenko can feel is rage. And he knows it's a rage he can easily bring to bear on Lump now. Lump looks weak and worn out, that's why he carries all the "tune-up" tools, it would be easy to even the score for Donnie, recalling the last time he saw Donnie. It was on the exit ramp with the sign around his neck. "Homeless – need help," no left hand and knows now it was Lump who put him there, made him homeless.

Lump reads Chenko's eyes, and pulls a knife, it doesn't bother Chenko at all, in fact Chenko welcomes it, it only adds to his rage. It would be like the pop bottle he always wanted to stick up Lump's ass.

But the ship afloat on the subsiding mixture inside him, that refused to sink in the uncertain seas, takes Chenko back to safe harbor and to what M T told him. "Any wound you receive here will not heal; any wound you give another here will not be forgotten."

He just looks at the villain for the last time and sees his wounds that refuse to heal, unwilling now to add to them. He gets up from the table and tells Lump he knows the guy looking for him, looks at the lighter and tells Lump "He wants it back." The reaction to these four words, were better than any punch Chenko could've thrown. Lump looks at the lighter and then Chenko and Chenko can see the look of doom in his eyes. He has no cards to play and has to fold, all hope lost.

"I'd get it to him if I were you." Chenko gets up and leaves the Slip Away, one of the few to get out that night. The sun is beginning to rise, the fresh air and activity on the street is a welcome relief as he walks to the corner leading back to the bridge.

On the corner of the bed, he continues with all he has to say to Ilene. "I'm walking towards you, always. When I come into view, you'll see me as I am, not as I was. Have a coin in my pocket for you. But seems you'll have to wait." I'm just as confused as you are. It's quite a journey I'm on."

******

For the first time Chenko wonders where he'll go once, he reaches the bridge, he has no idea which way to turn to get home. He realizes his destination hasn't changed, just the way to it, he doesn't know what forward is anymore. For the moment all he knows is his way to the bridge, it's a crapshoot from there.

This moment is overtaken by all that surrounds him and all he now knows. There's a certain amount of comfort where he is and with the people he's observed, but it's not total comfort, there's something more, but he has no idea what it is he wants or how to go about getting it. A feeling comes over him, he's in someplace he needs to be, but doesn't want to be.

As he walks towards the bridge he's greeted with smiles and nods, but nothing more. Those around him have reached some plateau where they're at a peace he can't find. In the best of ways, those around him let him know he doesn't belong where they are. They're kind and gentle in their responses to Chenko and if they offer any advice, it's to keep moving forward. They'll help him any way they can to get him home.

It's a strange situation. Chenko accepts their rejection with appreciation. He knows they're telling him the truth. It's a truth that can't be ignored, just as the shortages they work around can't be ignored. Somehow everyone here has learned to share them. All have learned to work with what they have, which isn't much, in harmony. What they don't have doesn't become a source of conflict, but a source of unity and there's the continual hope what turns up short won't last forever, increasing the joy of all when a shortage is eventually met.

The shortages exist to be overcome; all are patient in overcoming them. The appeal of this place isn't found in tremendous wealth, streets of gold, fountains and mansions, banquets, but in the tremendous harmony in making what once was what it is meant to be, without the bad behavior of wealth. Chenko is unable to process he's in a dimension within a dimension.

He gazes at the warehouses on the hill. Begins to wonder about all he's stolen and if those who surround him now, are the ones he stole from. He wonders if Lump's warehouse is up there and tries to guess which one it would be among the big and small, figuring it would be big, Lump stole a lot. Chenko stops looking and decides it really doesn't matter about other people's warehouses and makes a decision about his own warehouse.

First, he had no idea it existed and second, since he's been made aware he seems to have no use for it, so far all he's needed in this dimension has been provided. It's just a reflection to him of what once was. But to those around him in their dimension within his dimension, it's more. Not only this, he now has the opportunity to return all he stole with interest. The interest he ignored in another life. It's now clear to him why he wound up in this part of town. Why he was shown what he has and what those around him need.

He decides to head to his warehouse before going to the bridge. When he gets there, he finds a fist size rock and beats on the lock until it breaks and opens the doors. He goes in only to find what he needs to make a sign, finds a nice brush, can of paint and a four-by-eight sheet of plywood he once used in another life and writes IT'S ALL YOURS. He puts the sign in front of the warehouse and then resumes his walk to the bridge. M T doesn't have to show him all he stole.

Chenko makes his way out of the warehouse district and the bridge gradually comes into view, there's someone standing in the middle of it. Chenko knows who it is and walks towards M T. He has a lot to tell and ask M T. When they're face to face Chenko first tells M T "The package has been delivered." Second, he asks "Why an enemy instead of a friend?"

He'll also tell M T he doesn't need to see the warehouse anymore. M T will tell Chenko "Thanks. So, fate could become your friend and I know." But before M T tells him this, he tells Chenko some other things of importance.

Their conversation on the bridge begins with Chenko telling M T about all his experiences in this dimension. "You already know all I'm going to say, but I'm going to say it anyway." Chenko begins. By the time he's through, what comes out is he's lost and that the place he's in now, the more he thinks about it, might be the place to stay, he's starting to feel the fatigue of another life. He knows he doesn't fit in here, but maybe this would change, he's scared to move on.

M T directs Chenko's eyes to a kid skipping rocks on the river, the rock skips over the surface; two splashes are seen, on the third splash the stone sinks to the bottom. He gives Chenko a stone he pulls from his pocket and tells Chenko to throw it as far as he can from the bridge. The stone leaves his hand and both wait for a splash that never comes. M T tells Chenko "See all they told you is right. You don't want this to be like another life, stopping short of what you want to attain." Then out of nowhere M T tells Chenko "Come on, it's time to weigh in."

The two make their way off the bridge. M T gives Chenko credit for keeping what he was told to keep and not keeping what he was to give "I sent you to a place where all could've been lost. You had your moments, but when fate stepped in you faced up to him and did what had to be done." Both have their own version of what happened, Chenko argues the technicalities M T brings up on how it really unfolded. Pointing out to M T that these technicalities didn't change the outcome and Chenko is right.

As they continue towards the scales M T tries to ease the apprehensions Chenko has about not making weight. He tells Chenko what he's been through in this dimension is a mixture of every doubt one can have, it's effect like the drink he had at the Slip Away. "Wanting more when you don't need more. Some can handle it, some can't."

M T asks "What didn't you see here?" Most would answer. "Saw it all." Chenko begins to process and answers M T ... "Didn't see one hospital, funeral home, church, cemetery, police station, or bathroom. No dogs or cats or rats or elephants. No silly unicorn." M T likes Chenko's answer and jokes "That's all some people see here. You're fortunate. Some are all part of another life you won't see again; others part of a new life and you will see again."

Chenko goes on with other things he noticed in this dimension, how he was never hungry, but always had an appetite, never had to sleep but could, and how the smokes just kept getting better.

At this point M T tells Chenko "You don't remember me, but I remember you." He then asks Chenko to think of a time he was at Billy Kaloon's office. Chenko has no problem processing and answers M T "When I got my affairs in order."

M T tells Chenko "You're thinking inside the office. Think outside the office."

At this point Chenko recognizes Emmett, sees himself handing him a couple of bucks and telling him "It's Okay." Emmett reads Chenko's mind and tells him. "It's Okay." Returning the favor on much higher level in this dimension. This new knowledge is beyond any knowledge of another life. The scripture fulfilled.

M T points to the scale in the distance. As they come upon it Chenko can see it's a perfectly engineered fulcrum and beam. The middle of the beam rests on the fulcrum, at each end of the beam, three perfectly made chains hang down in perfect length from one point of origin and lead to three equally spaced points attached to a large disk, the disk at each end of the beam is in perfect balance with the other. Chenko looks at it, and feels like Christ going to the cross.

M T leads Chenko to a platform at one end of the beam, which is maybe ten feet above the disk. His broken and mangled body is brought out and put on the disk at the other end and the empty disk is raised to the platform and Chenko is told to step on to it.

He takes his final deep breath in this dimension and does as he's told. His weight is taken and known to everyone, but him. All he feels is his disk go down and stop; he can't see how it aligns with the flesh on the other disk. It's like being on elevator. When the disk stops and Chenko gets off, M T tells Chenko "When you wake up tomorrow, you'll be in a different place." This is all he says and then vanishes.

It's different for everyone in this dimension. This is how it went for Chenko. After M T disappears, he finds himself in the bedroom, now realizing he's been home all along. He continues all he has to say to Ilene. "I'm walking towards you, always. When I come into view, you'll see me as I am, not as I was. I have a coin in my pocket for you. But it seems you'll have to wait. I'm just as confused as you are. It's quite a journey I'm now on. While I'm on this journey, I want you to know the good in you, our children and all I know, outweighs the bad. Life has been fair to me thanks to all of you. We're separate now, but not forgotten, look for me in your memories and dreams, I'll be there. Promise."

He moves from the corner of the bed to lie down; he goes to sleep and leaves this dimension.

CHAPTER VII: ETERNITY

E veryone knows of eternity but who can explain it? No one on this side of the door. It's said to come in two flavors: good and bad. But even this is an unknown. Those who've tasted it have kept it to themselves after passing through the "arc of life." At best, it's a blending of the known with the unknown. The two don't mix to make a fact.

Eternity is the keystone wedged between faith and hope in the arch over the doorway to the unknown. The last word one sees passing through it. Even though eternity is a concept, it's treated as a fact. The beauty of eternity is everyone is entitled to their opinion and no one can be wrong, since no one on this side of the door really knows. The only fact eternity offers is those who say they know; in reality know no more than the next person.

If one thinks about it, eternity presents a host of problems we're not used to. For example, it's timeless; time is no longer a commodity one can run out of, it no longer has a function. Time marks the interval between beginning and end in our universe. The intervals are put together and we call it history, where one interval stops another begins. In eternity there's a beginning, but no end, all the history is the same. There'll be no past only present and future. Here everyone has a history, but in eternity? If history exists at all in eternity, it'll be different.

Perhaps eternity could be calculated by eliminating the constant "t" (time) in all our calculations governing the laws of physics and mathematics that explain our universe and recalculate. But to eliminate the function of time makes them unworkable; we don't have anything to replace time, there's no rational substitute. The laws of physics and mathematics that apply in this universe are different in a timeless universe. Time doesn't have a function in eternity; it might be hard to get used to, since time is all we know, all we understand.

These are just two examples (history and time) of many that may exist, pointing out some of the challenges eternity might present. Eternity, if it's anything, is a place of all possibilities. Possibilities that are beyond our comprehension, which Chenko is about to find out.

He's asleep on his bed and what would be called a dream is beyond a dream. There's no longer a boundary between real and imagined in what Chenko dreams and what he actually sees. They occur in unison and where once one would cancel the other out in reality, one would be greater than the other, in this sleep they blend together in a new dimension and imagination becomes reality. What Chenko would call a dream is the last experience he'll have with beginning and end. When he wakes up, he'll be in eternity, an eternity whose flavor is yet to be determined.

Where he now lays the process of his release from the tomb begins. It's an interesting process. The time Chenko spent in his dimension is only known to God, Chenko would think in terms of weeks instead of days if he were asked, but has no idea and never will. Either way, days or weeks, his time will fall within the interval of three days; see the old dimension of time evolves into a new dimension of time and changes what a day is in its dimension and perception. They're unknown days to us, but known days to God.

This evolution allows Chenko to be present at his calling hours, funeral, cremation and wake, even though he was in another place subject to a different dimension of time. His sleep brings on a dream that evolves into a vision of what took place in the dimension of the life he departed.

It would be a mistake for one to think what they learn about Ananias Zachenko is some insight on the end, that there is a pattern that can be followed here in explaining the unexplainable. You're only aware of all I tell you in this dimension. It bears repeating, the end is different for everyone. This is why it's not uncomfortable in letting you know how it worked out for one soul; no secrets of what is to come to you have been given away in what you've been told, even though you may think otherwise.

All that's been told so far is that time is arbitrary and a year has several different meanings depending on what you're measuring, there are calendar years, light years, dog years, for example. They've been mentioned, but there are more that haven't been mentioned, chronological years, physical years, mental years, to mention a few. It all comes down to age, the number of calendar, light, dog, or other types of year one used to determine age, for one reason or another, in life and to what end and for how long.

******

Calling hours, the process to attend is based on age and age here is the average of chronological years, physical years and mental years. One can attend their calling hours if their average age is between ten and ninety. At ten there are just enough years to capture one's impact on others. Beyond ninety there are enough years where this impact would escape, cases where others outlive one or one outlives others. Those under or over are excused and told of their calling hours later.

A weakness in any of the three brings the average down; strength in any of the three brings the average up. It's a paradox in life, a low average age makes one perceive themselves as young and youth is always preferred to the wisdom found in a high average and old age. Chenko is about to demonstrate the paradox and barely escape it.

Chenko has a chronological age of sixty-four, a physical age of seventy-one, due to his vices, and in the past where his mental age would've helped bring down his average age, now by virtue that he wasn't beginning to forget short term events in comparison to his peers, and before his illness wasn't on any medication, he's given one hundred twenty-nine. Chenko's average age is eighty-eight. Chenko is present when this calculation is made and so is M T. It's made by a group of people Chenko doesn't know and he questions them.

He begins in protest "What! Another three years and I'd be out of the picture to attend." Chenko points out to them he's never had that high a measurement in mental ability. It's like he's making an argument to be dumber than he is to lower his age, M T looks at him shaking his head. It's not enough to stop Chenko and he continues, eighty-eight will make me the oldest guy to show up!" M T whispers to him in a tone to let Chenko know he'd better back off. "Who are you?"

The group of three women and two men he and M T stand before, tell both they'll take what Chenko says into consideration. But before they do, they inform Chenko eighty-eight is the age he would've reached if he hadn't hit the sycamore and that he really doesn't want to get into a processing contest with them. There isn't a question he has that they can't answer and there are two ways they could go about this, Chenko could accept their number or they could go through proving each step taken to arrive at the number, one is better than the other. Chenko makes the right decision and accepts their number, but not without a sigh.

The agreement made, the group goes into caucus; Chenko and M T grab a smoke... "Forget age. This is the last time you'll ever use it." M T begins and continues "You're making this harder than it has to be. You've got some concepts to give up. There is no youth where you're going."

Chenko processes what he's being told and comes to a conclusion that surprises him, if he lived to eighty-eight it means he would've beaten his illness. Top of the dog year scale would've put him at seventy-one; the final age given beats his best estimate by seventeen years. It gives him a new outlook and with this outlook comes the last thought he ever has about his age. All of the sudden the age given is okay with him and the agreement totally acceptable, with what he knows now.

They finish their smokes and return to the group. A woman steps forward and begins to tell Chenko and M T they've considered Chenko's concerns about the age he'll be attending his calling hours; however, the age will not change. His age has been reaffirmed. But they will give him a noble appearance that will overcome the ill-fitting clothes he'll wear. He'll be offsetting in appearance. They'll give him a history that all can barely recall when he talks to them. He'll know more about them, than they will know of him, but most will be vaguely able to pull him in like some weak radio frequency. There also will be times he won't be allowed to speak.

He will be like some relative the family has heard about, but never seen. In their eyes he'll appear to be legitimate, he won't be viewed as a stranger, but he will be viewed as a mystery. He'll be allowed to bring up any memory. He'll be allowed to tell them places he's never been and things he's never done as if he had because of his age. M T will drop him off and pick him up. The more Chenko hears the more he likes the set up. M T tells him "Know what? ...Going to your calling hours will be your first taste of eternity. Let's make it good."

From here on out everything is turned over to M T. He's informed he'll be going along; it comes as surprise to him and like Chenko wants to question them, but accepts with a humble nod, his humility just short of covering up an expression on his face saying. "Why?" It goes unanswered. M T thought the deal was to drop him off and pick him up, but after more careful consideration the group thinks it would be a good idea he goes along. They have their reasons.

Chenko will be the mystery at his calling hours, M T will be the stranger. M T likes the set up. Chenko will answer many questions of others, but only asking others one question "Who's that guy over there?"

M T tells Chenko he has to take off for a while. "You can go to the Slip Away tavern if you want, but at sunrise be at the bridge. We'll leave from there." Chenko goes to the bridge.

The next morning M T shows up in a car that best could be described as a cross between a Chevy Monza and a Yugo. Chenko starts to laugh. "What is it a Mongo?" M T thinks for a moment of answering "No, it's a Yuza." Instead, he answers "Yeah, a Mongo. I like that."

"This isn't my first rodeo," M T explains. "I've been to calling hours before. No reason in the world you shouldn't be able find this car in any parking lot."

He didn't tell Chenko it took him more than one calling hour to take that card away from everyone. M T ends, "See, a lot of souls who go to their hours, funeral, wake get caught up in the people and surroundings and start ghosting. It's a pain in the ass, when they start doing this. I've already got two ghosting on me now. I have to check on, probably why they're sending me. Don't need a third, leaves a bad taste, you tracking?" Chenko nods.

After the warning the two drive off, the radio is turned on and Chenko and M T begin to debate who's better: The Beatles or the Stones? They plow through a dozen cream sticks and drink coffee M T picked up at the bakery, smoke and listen to the radio, heading to the Mountainford Funeral Home.

******

Ilene has gotten the message and will never forget being in the bedroom when she first heard it and what she found as she cleaned up the mess he made. How all she was going to tell him changed. It wasn't any different than what Chenko felt after hitting the sycamore.

When the realization hit her, she made no sound or movement, just cried. Overwhelmed with the feeling, it can't be, and the fact that it is. It's a devastation she's never known. All the harsh words between them now forgotten and every kind word remembered. It was no different for Eve and Hope when they are told.

It was rough at first, but all gained their composure when Ilene tells her children what she found that stopped her tears. She tells them how she was looking at the ceiling until she could bear it no longer; she was hoping to see him, but all she saw was a watery surface, the bulbs in the ceiling light burning like a fire and nothing more. When she looked down, she saw, between the dresser and their bed, on the carpet "Dad's Kopek."

The coin given Chenko by his father, a Russian coin, a double headed eagle on one side, the Tsar on the other side, dated 1776. The large copper coin all had been shown at one time or another. The coin that always was in his jewelry box, that hasn't been seen for years, now here it is on the floor. She ends her story "He's letting us know he's okay." She tells them "Billy Kaloon called soon after and everything is in order. He's left us more than this coin, but nothing worth as much as him and now this coin."

Mountainford receives his body. A casket is chosen, an obituary written and all the arrangements made, calling hours at the funeral home, funeral at the church, wake at the barn. The Mountainford's are friends of the family and make everything less challenging for the Zachenko's. Both families go back a long way.

Chenko's wife and children, brothers and sister, never see his remains at the funeral home, a few hours before it all starts, they are shown a casket with an American flag on it, Sonny and Jeep the only ones to have seen at the hospital what it holds. It's the first time his brothers and sister hear of his terminal illness.

The obituary had quite an impact, and appeared in the newspapers by mistake. Chenko got pneumonia a few years back, he took it the point he was in serious condition when they put him in the hospital. He missed a few Fridays and during his absence the Barnnites drafted an obituary for him. Thinking when they showed it to him, he'd pull through, which he did. Oddly enough Chenko kept it and put it with the will.

Billy Kaloon showed it to Ilene, letting her know it wasn't a condition and that he'd treat it more as a request. Billy had read it and after Ilene read it, they agreed it was pretty much the truth, but it isn't going in the papers. After seeing Billy, she went to the funeral home to drop off some pictures, somehow the obit they removed from Chenko's file is put in with the pictures.

She put the stack of pictures and the obit under them on a corner of the desk, gets into a long conversation about the pictures with Connie Mountainford. They went through all of them. It was good, they had some laughs. Connie in the end looking at the stack they put back on top of the obit asks "Obit?" Ilene answering "Yes," Ilene taking her question as the last thing that still has to be done and that she'll e-mail it tonight, but doesn't say this, still lost in the memories, thinking she has said this.

After Ilene leaves, picking up only her purse and some paperwork from Connie, Connie begins to type in the barely legible writing on some faded notebook paper in an e-mail to the newspaper. The whole time feeling it unusual and unexpected, but this is what Ilene left.

She reads it from the screen more than a few times. At first, she doesn't know what to think, but each time she reads it she likes it a little more. Each time she reads it a little more of Chenko comes out between the lines. Whoever wrote it, knew him and although it's not Ilene's writing, she can't be ruled out as a suspect as to its origin. This is the main body of what is sent:

Ananias Ezra Zachenko

Ananias, who was born June 15th, 1948 and died about two days before the date of this newspaper, showed us all good fortune does exist. In the Army he was in line to become a general, fortunately the line was long. In business he was involved in many high-level projects; fortunately, the involvement was short lived.

He was kind to animals until they annoyed him and then became another person. He was frugal with his money, but generous with others. He had an energy that followed the path of least resistance. He had a few more vices than virtues. Any goal he went after became an all or nothing venture, outcomes skewed towards nothing. His memberships include the human race.

Though he was not naturally honest, he was so sometimes by chance. And nine out of ten times you ran into him he had a full heart and clear eyes, took advantage of few and helped most. Had a truck he'd let anybody use. He was an easy mark for the homeless on any street. Actually, he had a pretty nimble mind and although the world will be less confusing without him, it won't be the same. So long Mind Bruiser.

Connie types who preceded him in death and who survives, when and where the calling hours, funeral and wake will take place. They're the last things she types in. For a moment she thinks of calling Ilene and knows she shouldn't hit the "send" button, but the phone rings and she gets tangled up in a problem over a shipment of coffins, the conversation is long and frustrating. Somewhere along the line, she hits the button, to feel like she's accomplishing at least something.

Later on, when she gets Ilene's e-mail, she realizes she's made a big mistake. Ilene and Connie eventually work this out between themselves and in the end, if anything; the obit that made the paper brings a lot of people out of the woodwork.

It doesn't go unmentioned, especially by those who read it more than once. Ilene never gives a direct answer when asked if she wrote it. Neither do Eve and Hope, but have considered taking credit. The more the Barnnites are mentioned, the more they deny it, just for fun. The author remains anonymous. Connie says nothing. To Connie's benefit, Ilene receives more than a few compliments on it. Especially by those who could read between the lines.

When Chenko and M T pull into the parking lot, they have trouble finding a parking spot. Chenko is smiling at the turn out, M T looks at him and says "I'm warning you." The smile doesn't go away.

But M T has some tricks up his sleeve. M T will tune him up. Once inside Chenko won't know him, he'll appear as he looks now to Chenko, but when Chenko points him out to others, asking who he is; M T will be another person. It will cause others to say "I don't know, but weren't you just talking to him?" M T will make him feel some of the senility that comes with his age, to keep him in line. Not only this, but he makes it so Chenko has to give the maximum effort in every step he takes, this also comes with his age. He'll tune him up; he'll be made to run like he should at eighty-eight.

M T tells Chenko before they go in. "Been waiting for this." He goes to the trunk and pulls out a large mirror, that defies explanation as to how it ever fit in the trunk, and for the first time since the sycamore Chenko sees his reflection. He has a thick shock of white hair on the edge of needing a haircut, combed straight back, his face has deep lines, but good color, tan, unblemished, and his eyes are as clear and as blue as they were the day he was born. He smiles even more when he sees his face. He's not far from the wizard look. But the smile goes away when he sees how he's dressed.

Chenko is wearing a wrinkled pinstriped searsucker coat. The collar on his light patterned plaid shirt is about three sizes too big, the tie hanging from it beyond description. The pants are a light green and bunched around the waist, with the one end of his belt hanging down about six inches at his crotch. They're also about two inches too short, showing his sagging navy blue socks. Well one is navy blue, the other black. His shoes are white sneakers that have Velcro straps instead shoelaces. This is how his now one hundred forty-five pounds frame is attired. He's dressed every bit his age and Chenko realizes this and shakes his head. He's gone from the wizard look to the clown look. M T chuckles and disappears.

Inside Chenko becomes Ezra Zachenko's cousin, Ananias. He'll be perceived this way. The two cousins covered a lot of ground on two continents during some pretty rough times, when fighting was plenty and food scarce. In fact, he was the reason that Helene met little resistance in naming their son Ananias. Also, the reason Ananias wasn't Ezra's first choice.

The two knew each other a little too well. Chenko wasn't named after him; there have been at least three or four over the history of the family. Ez always pointed this out. Helene, that Ananias opened St. Paul's eyes. No Ananias, no St. Paul. Even though neither parent claims the cousin as Chenko's namesake there have always been rumors of the opposite.

Ezra's cousin Ananias was a character of family lore, someone heard about, but never seen. He came to America with Ez, stayed awhile and then went to the Yukon, owned a lumber yard. Relatives used to ask Ez if Nye was named after his cousin. He'd always answer "Ananias is a family name." They loved getting him in to a conversation about his cousin. Both he and his cousin had quite a reputation in their youth. Helene dreaded these conversations when her children and her nieces and nephews were around. It was Ez's cousin Ananias who gave Ez the coin, Ez gave it to his son, Ananias.

Chenko shuffles into the Mountainford Funeral Home. He stands in line to sign the book on a podium leading to the room where his coffin is. There are very few people he doesn't know, he can't wait to talk to them; he's like a kid who's just been released for recess, the funeral home, like a playground. M T watches him and enjoys how he waves and nods at people who have no idea who he is. After signing the book, he gets in the receiving line.

It gets more entertaining for M T. While in line Chenko stops Sneaky, by grabbing his arm as he walks by and with big smile tells him. "Want to talk to you later!" Unaware, Sneaky sees him as some old guy Sneaky doesn't know. Sneaky politely nods. Chenko tells him, "And don't be switching any cards on the flowers. You know, replacing someone's with yours."

This surprises Sneaky into an unexpected nervous laugh and he can't help telling Chenko. "Oh. We'll talk!" He looks at those around who might have heard their conversation and rolls his eyes, knowing Chenko's age and appearance work to his benefit. But it's not enough to take away the intrigue of how this old guy knows the trick he likes to say he pulls at these events, even though he's never done it.

When he's received by Ilene, Eve and Hope he's unable to speak, the only thing he can do is shake their hand and look at them with tears in his eyes. He becomes the kind old man, who can only express himself this way and because of his age, it is all he has to do to be accepted and appreciated. Chenko doesn't expect this; he has so much to tell them, but isn't allowed to speak to them. When he gets to his brothers and sister, he's able to give them a fascinating introduction as to who he is.

Sonny, Jeep and Helene take him to a chair given up by one of Chenko's nephews. Chenko surprises them by telling his nephew "Thanks Ivan." He becomes someone they definitely want to talk to. He's asked to stay and when the line ends, they will be right back. This is when M T lets Chenko see him for the first time.

He's standing across the room giving Chenko a wry smile. And for the first time Chenko feels like this guy knows everything about him, but he's a stranger. He looks away from M T for a moment and when he returns his gaze to where he stood M T is gone. Chenko for a while becomes preoccupied with knowing where he is at all times, where he sees him changes from moment to moment.

As Chenko waits for the receiving line to end, he tunes into all the conversations around him while continually hunting down M T. He becomes aware of the rumors starting to circulate about his terminal illness. It takes him back to his diagnosis when he set his agenda. He completed the first phase, but not the last two. He sees himself saying "Second will be the relationships, which will involve visitations, conversations and conclusions."

With this visitation he realizes the whole second phase is now unfolding in front of his eyes, there's plenty of conversations and conclusions being made now. He continues his thoughts: "Third will be the heroic act which will involve assessments, decisions and actions." The rumors now starting to point to assessments, decisions and actions he didn't make, which some are beginning to think he did.

He's approached by a stranger who was standing next to him in the receiving line who tries to engage him in a conversation. Having heard who is supposed to be. In the middle of the questions he's being asked, Chenko stops the stranger with a question of his own "I'm sorry, but who's the guy standing over there?" Having pinned down M T. When the stranger looks, he sees Sneaky and answers "I don't know, but weren't you just talking to him?" Chenko suspects this person is beyond anyone he knew in life.

Chenko's brothers and sister return as soon as they can. Ilene, Eve and Hope are engaged in a conversation with a man unwilling to let them go. It's Linwood Sharlitin and he's rewarding each of them by giving them his card. He's unrelenting in his condolences to the point Jeep is ready to go over and show him the door, but is waved off by Ilene. He tells Ilene of the business he and Chenko conducted and the ministry he's formed as if Chenko was somehow involved. His ministry is where he belongs and Chenko was a big part of getting him there. Ilene is polite, but knows better.

When the conversation ends, she and the girls come over to shake Chenko's hand once more and excuse themselves to go home, they're exhausted. Chenko is heartbroken. Later on, when Ilene finds out about Linwood's ministry and the "new Chenko" his ministry created, she puts him where he belongs – in a cell.

Chenko tells his brothers and sister things only he and they would know. He talks of letters that went back and forth between him and their mother. He always wrote once every two or three years to both Ezra and Helene, Helene would always answer them. This is how he knows so much about them; he brings up the "ivy incident." He tells them of the coin he gave their father. When they tell Ilene, Eve and Hope the following day, all wish they'd have stayed and given more than kind and gentle smiles to the old man who turned out to be such a pleasant mystery.

When they ask Chenko where he's staying, he answers them with the surprised look a person his age might give. "I don't know." M T shows up using his most angelic personality as he explains he brought the old man and is in charge of watching him. He's masterful in answering all questions and leaving no doubt Chenko is in the best of hands. Again, Chenko is unable to speak, and is turned over to M T.

It's not until they reach the Mongo that Chenko recognizes M T. M T feels good about the calling hours, Chenko showed few signs of ghosting on him, but realizes there's still the funeral, cremation and wake, he's not out of the woods yet. The two drive off to a kitchen that never closes and talk about the calling hours.

******

Through the night and into the morning Chenko and Emmett eat, drink, smoke and talk. They share a table with another man and are waited on by a young woman. Just like appetite has replaced hunger, sleep is no longer required, but enjoyed, there's no fatigue to its onset; one goes to sleep at their pleasure. The atmosphere of where they are only enhances the clarity of where they will go from here.

At first Chenko mentions the obit and his surprise it made the papers. There was talk at the calling hours it happened by mistake, but even so, it struck Chenko as strange it got in, no matter what the circumstances. Ilene would share the thought. She's not there, but where she is, this would be a common ground for both of them. Chenko not knowing it came as just as big a surprise to her as to him when she found out.

Chenko tells M T "Not that I mind it. Just surprised it got by Ilene." M T knows exactly how it happened, but answers "Maybe it didn't. Maybe it was meant to be." Chenko shrugs in response, still on the fence. M T plays his second card, pulls out an eight slash Zippo Storm King and lights a smoke then exhales. "Fate," Chenko nods, lost in thought about the lighter he just saw. They talk about it for a moment and move on to other subjects. M T will let Ilene tell Chenko how the mistake was made. That time will come.

M T tells Chenko they'll go to the funeral, he'll be seen, but Chenko won't. But before he goes into detail, he shares some observations with him on the calling hours. "Think about all the people who'll be asking questions about you. You got to see them. They got to see you. You know who they are, but they don't know who you are...You think they do, but they don't. They're asking questions."

It's almost like M T is letting him on a little secret. M T ends "Just about everyone shows up at their calling hours and no one knows. They're into their memories, not you; this is what you are now. A memory. Even though you're standing right in front of them."

Funerals are solemn affairs. M T points this out to Chenko. "Not much room for irreverence at the final goodbye." He adds "It will be like when you hit the sycamore and the crews cleaned up and reported what happened, with you there, but not there... Only this time it won't be new." He lets Chenko know before they go, he's looking for some answers and starts out. "You chose a church. Before we go inside, tell me about your chess game with God."

Chenko leans over a cup of coffee, takes a sip, looks up and asks M T for a light, smiles when he sees the lighter, leans back in his chair and in a white cloud of smoke answers "What you want to know?"

M T doesn't answer; instead, he just nods for Chenko to continue. Chenko tells him he'll be as honest in what he says, as Christ is with him.

"I'm a Believer, but not a Christian. I don't have a problem being a Believer, just being a Christian. I haven't attained it. I don't take it lightly calling myself one; it's too many things to too many people who call themselves Christians who just make it an overworked word. Sure, it's the same way for some guys in other religions too,"

Chenko continues in a rapid fire mode. "To be honest, if it's all about what I'm hearing on the radio and seeing on TV, cherry picking the Bible verses about tamped down shares, love gifts, anointments, raptures (the word doesn't even appear in the Bible), prayer warriors, and hearing and seeing those dressed in their artificial wealth, who take every word of the Book literally instead of spiritually, who only know how to tell me to go to my phone so they can get another satellite dish so more people can see them, I'm not interested. Buying into them was a move I didn't take."

At the table Chenko sees all he wants to say in increasing clarity. He talks for a while about conversions, where one religion can't hold a soul and that soul looks to another. How religion in general is like being on the used car lot, trying to pick out the best ride for down the road. Everyone with their own owner's manual to be followed literally, that can't be deviated from, or nothing gets fixed. No room for innovation.

Chenko points out if he were born in another part of the world, odds are he'd be under a different religion; the birthright is too geographical, each religion wants to take over the other. Some look for converts from the other, some want to eliminate the other. He points out it's all very confusing to him. If it weren't for the spare of "spirituality" in the trunk, he doubts he would've gotten this far. Seems to him those making the pitch are more interested in their own word of God, than the spirit of God.

At this point Chenko surprises M T; it's the first and only time this happens. He tells M T "I've seen the sixty-three books and done some cherry picking too." He adds that the obit wasn't the only piece of paper in the folder with his will. He has the five scriptures from the New Testament that had, still have and always will have, the most impact on him from the Father, Son and Holy Ghost.

There is no doubt Ilene got them and they'll be read at his funeral. It puts M T in the position to see if what he's being told will come to pass and he knows the group that lets this happen. Chenko ends "These are the five pieces on the board I never gave up."

In another life Chenko was capable of reciting the long narrative of the *Cremation of Sam Magee* in a fluid and almost flawless manner. He did it many times. All he is about to recite next is for the first time and is flawless in its presentation as he begins to tell M T how honest Christ is with him. He asks M T "Want to know how honest?" and recites Matthew 10:34-39 word for word.

"Do not think that I have come to bring peace on earth; I have not come to bring peace, but a sword. For I have come to set a man against his father, and a daughter against her mother, and a daughter-in-law against her mother-in-law; and a man's foes will be those of his own household. He who loves father or mother more than me is not worthy of me; and he loves son or daughter more than me is not worthy of me; and he who does not take up his cross and follow me is not worthy of me. He who finds his life will lose it, and he who loses his life for my sake will find it.

At the end of the recitation Chenko notes "It's pretty upfront. A good piece not to give up." Tells M T it's a hard piece of scripture and true. He then confesses he put his cross down as much as he picked it up. There were times he didn't take it up at all or follow and because of this; he doesn't know what he's lost or what he'll find. "And this is being honest."

Chenko feels more coherent than ever and unable to stop. "I have another piece still on the board." He goes on to tell M T his appreciation of this piece comes in the authority of faith that gives faith its power. Romans and Jews hated each other, yet one hated points out the power of faith to the ones who hate him. It's a gift. Faith among friends is easy, but faith among enemies hard. But when enemies find it can be shared, faith is in its full dimension of the authority behind it and becomes a power. It's a designed authority that allows it to move with speed and hit with impact. Chenko asks M T "Want to see how it works?" He recites Matthew 8:5-11 word for word.

...As he entered Caper'na-um, a centurion came forward to him, beseeching him and saying, "Lord, my servant is lying paralyzed at home, in terrible distress." And he said to him, "I will come and heal him." But the centurion answered him "Lord I am not worthy to have you under my roof; but only say the word and my servant will be healed. For I am a man under authority, with soldiers under me; and I say to one, 'Go,' and he goes, and to another, 'Come,' and he comes, and to my slave, 'Do this,' and he does it." When Jesus heard him, he marveled, and said to those who followed him, "Truly, I say to you, not even in Israel have I found such faith."

Chenko ends. "I'm thinking the Roman centurion was beyond any differences when he saw Christ and the Jews there saw him differently after he did. But only say the word and my servant will be healed. And it happened." All because of faith. The authority behind faith that gives it its power. I still have this piece."

For the times Chenko put down his cross he tells M T it was hope that let him pick it up again. He talks of what he learned from the crucifixion, how it shows the nature of man and the character of man. Christ between two criminals one showing the nature, the other the character, one giving up hope, the other finding it. Chenko knowing he's been a criminal of nature to avoid justice and a criminal of character accepting justice, but knows he's been more of one than the other. He takes a long hit from his cigar and begins to recite Luke 23:39-43 word for word.

One of the criminals who were hanged railed at him, saying, "Are you not the Christ? Save yourself and us!" But the other rebuked him, saying, "Do you not fear God, since you are under the same sentence of condemnation? And we indeed justly; for we are receiving the due reward of our deeds; but this man has done nothing wrong." And he said "Jesus, remember me when you come into your kingly power." And he said to him, "Truly, I say to you, today you will be with me in Paradise."

He tells M T "I've always had the hope of a criminal." Don't know how many times I've come close to losing this piece. But it's still on the board."

Although he's still capable of reciting more scripture word for word, he paraphrases the last two that had an impact on him. He tells M T he doesn't have a problem about the way the judgment is made and talks of the scripture before Matthew 25:45, the part about how we treat those who are always with us, the hungry, naked, those in prison, sick and poor. Tells M T there's a little Christ in all us, it's the part that lets us know how we've been treated and how we've treated others. Know what He's going to say, then recites Matthew 25:45... *Then he will answer them; "Truly, I say to you, as you did it not to one of the least of these, you did it not to me.*

Chenko ends, "I've helped some people up. Knocked some down, and on the board, I've always tried to remember to use this piece."

Finally, Chenko winds down telling M T about his chess game with God and the pieces he never gave up, that are still on the board: honesty, faith, hope, judgment. M T is eager to tell Chenko he still owes him one more scripture, but Chenko is a step ahead of him. M T for the first time feels his mind has been read. Before he can ask, Chenko recites First Thessalonians 5:02: *For you yourselves know well that the day of the Lord will come like a thief in the night.* Chenko continues "All those Bible Thumpers on the radio and TV, who love traveling through *Revelations* and love telling everyone about their travels, stay away from this scripture. There is more money in John's dream than the *Word.*" Ends by telling M T, "He sure came like a thief in the night when I hit that sycamore. End of the world for me."

They get up from the table, the man sitting with them drinking endless cups of coffee, smiles and nods, the young waitress also smiles and says goodbye. They push their chairs under the table, leave the kitchen and enter the church. The pushing, leaving and entering all occur at the same moment.

Next thing Chenko sees is the light coming through the stain glass windows and all its colors falling on the coffin in front of the Altar. People come in and speak in quiet voices, once seated they become silent, it is a solemn affair. Pastor Brown begins the service by reading the *Apostles Creed:*

I believe in God the Father Almighty Maker of Heaven and Earth and in His only Son Jesus Christ our Lord. Conceived by the Holy Spirit, born of the Virgin Mary, suffered under Pontius Pilate, was crucified dead and buried.

The third day He arose from the dead; he ascended into heaven, and sitteth at the right hand of God the Father Almighty; from thence he shall come to judge the quick and the dead.

I believe in the Holy Spirit, the holy catholic Church, the communion of Saints, the forgiveness of sins, the resurrection of the body and the life everlasting.

Eulogies are given by his brothers and sister. A brief sermon is given by Pastor Brown, telling all Chenko had his cross with him in the end. Between the eulogies the other scriptures are read. M T asks why there was no mention of the *Apostles Creed* and Chenko tells him it isn't scripture.

M T appears silent, but is engaged in conversation as they sit in the back and talk to each other with no one hearing them. M T is touched by the service and tells Chenko, "You got a lot tears from those who'll miss you."

He lets Chenko know he won't be going to the cremation (everyone does that solo) and that he'll be at the wake, but Chenko will only see him once, at the end. The group has granted M T optional powers. M T tells Chenko... "I'll give you one for each scripture." Chenko will be allowed to appear five times to whomever he chooses, other than Ilene, Eve and Hope. But those he chooses will eventually tell his family. He ends in afterthought. "The cremation and wake, don't start ghosting on me." M T vanishes and Chenko heads to the crematorium.

******

It will be the first time in the old dimension that Chenko is alone. He finds he has to physically move to get where he wants. He can no longer seemingly appear where he wants to be. For the most part he can't be seen, heard, or felt, but has weight.

He slides in the passenger's side of the hearse and waits for the driver. He sits there feeling like he did in another life; the trip to the crematorium feels like a trip to the dentist who's heavy on the drill and light on the Novocain. Or like right before a doctor sets a broken bone; the trip to the principal's office for some whacks; going to basic training; sent home from work and almost fired. Allthe stuff one had to go through to get better; he wasn't a stranger to any of them and feels the crematorium won't be any different.

The driver gets in; he's in his late twenties, well-groomed and partied out from the night before. In the mood to relax, now that this is the last thing he has to do, get Chenko thirty miles down the road. After two miles he's out of his boss's view and loosens his tie and turns on the radio. He takes out a smoke, it's a joint, and fires it up. Chenko just laughs and shakes his head, sees himself at the same age. Then starts to think this guy and this situation, both tailor made for him in another life and the feeling starts to overtake him. He begins to ghost.

Chenko doesn't think he can do it, but tries and is surprised when it works. The driver sings along with Randy

Newman's *You Can Leave Your Hat On,* he's really on it in his private karaoke. Right in the middle of the song the station mysteriously changes, and the driver becomes lost in the endless rifts of *Anna Godivita.*

He shakes his head, looks at the station on the radio, and changes it back and laughs, "Pretty good weed." Chenko is amused, but changes the station one too many times, to where the driver just thinks the scanner is stuck. Chenko finds a station that's playing polkas, leaves it on the station and if the driver changes it, changes it right back, if he turns the radio off, Chenko turns it back on, then he starts playing with the volume.

The first time Chenko maxes out the volume, the driver fires up a normal smoke to take the edge off. He throws the pack on the dashboard; it slides towards Chenko after a sharp right-hand turn. Chenko puts the pack in the glove box, wedges it in the large clear plastic envelope holding the owner's manual; sticks it between the pages, like some kid trying to hide a pack from his parents. It goes unnoticed by the driver, who at the same time loses his smoke when he tries to flick the ashes out the cracked passenger window. By accident it blows right out of his hand, only got about three hits. The window is cracked because the air is on max; Chenko begins to play with temperature controls as soon as he makes the connection.

The need for tobacco overcomes the driver and he looks on the dash for his smokes, then the floor, but can't find them. It bothers him to the point he makes an unauthorized stop at a McDonald's and pulls into an open spot in the parking lot and begins to search in earnest. It's a new pack and they aren't cheap.

While he tears the inside of the hearse apart Chenko bounces up and down in his seat. All the driver sees is the surface of passenger seat sink down and then back up to its original position, like the seat is having a spasm.

It momentarily stops the search, but he then continues; nothing is overlooked; he's locked into the search. Finally, he finds the pack and says to himself "What is going on?" Then rationalizes he's stoned. What he realizes is that everything happening isn't happening, when in fact it is. He lights a smoke, feels the sweat on his forehead, shakes his head again and turns the temperature control off max heat back to max air.

Chenko would've kept this up all the way to their destination, but they pass his old high school and it triggers a memory. Actually, it's a new high school, the one he went to was torn down, but all he sees is the old high school. The memory unfolds when he realizes he's now in a hearse and driving by it for the last time, going to the "big heater." Knowing what's in store, he tries to find some memories of the coldest he's ever been, to make the final destination a little more palatable, but can't find any. All that comes back is two long narrative poems he learned in the old building.

The assignment was made in an English class, a long narrative poem had to be memorized and given the class. Each chose their poem to recite in front of the class. The assignment would be the major grade for the six- week period. The reason Chenko learns two long poems is that his first choice is rejected by Miss May. Her class was not ready for James Whitcomb Riley's; *The Passing of the Backhouse.* His brother Sonny suggests it. The poem begins this way:

When memory keeps me company and moves to smiles or tears,

A weather-beaten object looms through the mist of years,

Behind the house and barn it stood, a half a mile or more,

And hurrying feet a path had made, straight to its swinging door.

Its architecture was a type of simple classic art.

But in the tragedy of life, it played a leading part...

It was a shame, Chenko had the lengthy poem memorized in two days, word for word; he liked it that much. Especially the part, how in the winter it had a seat so cold it would make a Spartan sob and the flies from there fly around mother's pies. The part where it's told, "they didn't tarry or linger long on what they left behind." It just got better as it went along.

But when his time comes to give his preliminary reading, during a study hall he's excused from, Miss May is amused, but not to the point where he can recite it to the class. She gives him a left-hand compliment after rejecting him, telling him the poem is college, not high school level. It's the mid-Sixties, Chenko begins to protest. The protest has nothing to do with censorship, although he couches it this way, but more in the fact he doesn't want to do anymore work, which he keeps to himself. Miss May senses this, but is firm in her decision. Within a day he comes up with Robert Service's *The Cremation of Sam Magee*, which she accepts.

He looks at the high school and recalls it all; he did twice the work for the grade, but did get an "A." This memory's surfacing is directly tied to where he's headed. The reason behind trying to remember the coldest he's ever been. Those memories won't come, although he knows they're there, all that comes back to him is the second poem he learned. It began:

There are strange things done in the midnight sun

By the men who moil for gold;

The Arctic trails have their secret tales

That would make your blood run cold;

The Northern Lights have seen queer sights,

But the queerest they ever did see

Was that night on the marge of Lake Lebarge

I cremated Sam McGee.

Now Sam McGee was from Tennessee, where the cotton blooms and blows.

Why he left his home in the South to roam 'round the Pole, God only knows.

He was always cold, but the land of gold seemed to hold him like a spell;

Though he'd often say in his homely way that "he'd sooner live in hell."

In a moment of true reflection with frightening overtones, he's feeling it's not like hell is out of the picture, Chenko wonders for the first time since the sycamore if this is where he is headed. This is the part of a dream everyone experiences, the bad part. The part that makes one want to wake up.

After passing the "old" high school, the thought comes and goes as the hearse pulls into the crematorium. The guy handling the inside is like the driver; in fact, he was with him the other night. They're work buddies, two of a kind. The driver starts out "What a trip!" Then starts telling the guy about the radio, heater, smokes, glove box, everything. The guy answers "Your rider spookin' on ya? Happens to me all the time around here." The driver answers "Nah, I think it's the weed." The guy answers "Yeah, I know it's the weed, that's what keeps it real." It gets to the point that Chenko can't listen to the nonsense anymore and walks inside to get away from them.

It's when the guy tells the driver "C'mon, let's get this slug over to the oven." Chenko is hit by the finality of this old dimension. He doesn't even have time for a final smoke as the driver and the guy wrestle the coffin forward. "This is it," he whispers to himself. In this moment he has to decide to stay outside the box and try to stay in this old dimension or crawl in it and try to get to a new dimension.

He crawls in and what takes place is still something he is unable to speak of as he's reduced to ash. When it's over he feels no weight, he feels like he's out of the dentist chair, the bone set, whacks taken, basic training over and he's back to work. His experience with beginning and end over. He floats over to his wake.

******

Chenko comes upon the barn towards night fall. He floats to it on the wind, like a kite tethered to an endless length of string. He effortlessly glides over the tree line to the ground. He hits the spot where he parked when hunting the Blue Jay. The jay is still there and laughs at him. It's good to be back and he can spend the night. In less than twenty-four hours his wake will take place.

The barn is the second place he'd rather be, first is home, but is unable to move in its direction, he's tried. Second place is really close to first and he's happy to be there. He moves inside and stops to look at the vanity he was working on. It's not where he left it; it's up against the wall. The place has been cleaned up. Chenko thinks it's the cleanest he's ever seen it.

He opens a drawer and sees whoever moved it put his tools in it. He's able to pick up a file. In this dimension the file appears to be floating in the air. For a few moments the file goes to work on the edge of the last piece of the new hardware he was making, the file and the hardware the only things that can be seen, not in hand or at rest, but floating in the air.

GM is taking an early evening walk and decides to go to the barn; he'll check it out before tomorrow's festivities. He feels obligated and it's an easy obligation to carry out for his friend's family. He stops and watches a kite float in the sky; it's hard to see off in the distance and goes down by the barn. Laughs and thinks the tree line got it. He'll look for it when he gets there.

He turns to see if the pilot is behind him, but no one is there. As he walks, he becomes occupied with how far away he is from the tree line where the kite disappeared. At least a half mile he thinks. When he turns around, he can see clearly another half mile over the wheat behind him and no one is there.

It perplexes him, whoever put the kite up also let out a mile or more of string and wonders if that's possible. GM aligns himself in the direction he last saw the kite, knowing it was under tension before it dropped from view, and starts to look on the ground for the string.

The string is found. GM bends down and looks in both directions and sees neither person nor kite. He finds a branch and spends some time breaking it in two. Thinking how when he was Chenko's age he could still snap the branch like a twig. While catching his breath he thinks of that age and mutters, "Hell, he had another twenty-five years."

He breaks out his pocket knife and cuts the string, it's hard to cut, and it has to be expensive, finds a fist size rock, and pounds a stake to mark one end. Throws the rock down; then picks up the other part of the branch and the other end of the string. He'll use it to wind the string around heading to the barn.

At first, it's easy, but in a short time it becomes cumbersome, as the ball of string grows rapidly. After a while GM abandons the idea. The huge ball of string is dropped in a field of wheat and not found until harvest time, when he has to pull it out of all the moving parts it bound up in his harvester. It will make him think of Chenko again and remind him of his walk. When he gets to the tree line, he can't find the kite.

At the barn Chenko moves into his office and looks out the window at the tree line. He remembers the last time he sat there, feeling like some old sheriff getting ready to track down an outlaw and wonders if that outlaw will show up at the wake.

He'll save an appearance in case he does. He's struck when he realizes he was hunting someone when he left this dimension. Thinking it might be the real cause to where he is now sitting. It's not good weight. He reaches for a cigar and a shot of whiskey like then, but the Dickel is in the freezer. He leaves the office to get it the moment GM comes into view.

He gets the Dickel, but can't find a glass, now that the place has been cleaned. While looking for one he gets sidetracked by the vanity again. He takes a pull from the bottle, and can't understand why he has the feeling he should finish the vanity, one last piece to file down and put on. He decides he could do this and he goes to work. He begins like always, by lighting his cigar and looking at the hardware and vanity deciding how he'll approach the work at hand.

It's at this point M T shows up. He's as unseen by Chenko, as Chenko is unseen by others. He's not in love with what he's seeing, if what Chenko is doing isn't ghosting, he doesn't know what is. But he decides to let him continue for other reasons. Besides he's interested to see if anyone notices it during the wake.

Chenko, on the other hand, never thinks of what he's doing as leaving a sign. He has some unknown reason it has to be finished and as unknown as it is, it won't leave him. M T will let him get the piece on, but not without some interruptions. He opens the man door to the barn and leaves it open. It goes unnoticed by Chenko as he picks up tool and part and again goes to work.

The angle GM takes to the barn allows him to see from a distance the door is open. Not a car on the place and the door was shut and locked when he checked it in the early morning. He decides to circle around the barn to one of the windows before he goes in. He finds one and crouches to give no more a target than he has to, only his eyes can be seen above its sill, keeping a very low profile taught from experience.

When he looks in, he sees the file and hardware move through the air, the filings falling like some magic dust to the floor. A cigar is picked up from the edge of the work table, then a cloud of smoke. The file and piece are put down and a bottle of Dickel is raised, tipped back, the fluid whiskey goes out of the bottle to nowhere. Everything stops for a while and then starts up again.

GM watches for a long time. M T lets what's going to happen next unfold. He tones down some of Chenko's appearance power, knowing it's not time for GM to enter his dimension, which is starting to happen. Knowing the RPM's of the thoughts running through his mind brought him close to red lining his mental tachometer.

GM returns to sitting below the window with his back against the barn, driven to the position by what he's seen.

He sits there like some soldier trying to decide if he should attack or retreat, overcome by wondering what will happen next. He's hit with the fact this is no Walt Disney movie, what he's seen is real and as much as he wants to doubt all of it, he can't. Even though it's a friend in the barn and not a foe, the proposition is still frightening, as he thinks "What if he's changed?" He's a prisoner of the thoughts about the dead in this dimension. "What if all he remembers is what he doesn't like about me?" GM thinks. He has no way of knowing.

The last thought comes and goes, and when it's gone, GM, on impulse, finds his feet and rushes the door no different than when he was nineteen in "the boot" (Italy), bursting through the doorway yelling "Chenko!" like some paratrooper yelling "Geronimo!"

Not knowing what he'd find once he hit the door, him not knowing what he'd find once inside, but now ready for anything. If it were possible, his entrance scares Chenko to death, M T laughs at Chenko's reaction once Chenko realizes this is no longer an option and what it really does is scare him to "appearance." An appearance Chenko hadn't planned on. Chenko has his appearances planned and GM isn't in the plan, but then none of the others planned for will get an appearance, except one.

It takes Chenko almost all of the night to appear to GM. Once he starts, he can't stop. This is because M T forgets for a while that he's toned down the power of appearance in Chenko. For a while the conversation between GM and Chenko might as well have taken place in two different rooms. Chenko is able to see and hear GM, but GM can do neither and is working off gut instinct. GM tells Chenko "I know you're here."

Chenko begins to power up an appearance and it's like trying to start Old Red when the battery was weak. There are times when it almost catches, but then fades out and you have to wait a few minutes before trying again.

Chenko is getting drained in his attempts to let GM know he's right. He is there. Frustration is setting in; he decides to pick up a hammer as a sign. It's a poor choice and spooks GM. But then he's hit with a brainstorm. He goes to his office and writes a note, "I'm here."

He returns to a wandering GM whose reminiscing about the crop circle. The more he talks the more comfortable he's becoming. GM offers up his hope for Chenko. "May you be in heaven an hour before the devil finds out you're dead."

The note is placed on the work bench by the door. It's a coin toss that GM sees it on the way out. He heads for the door, but fate doesn't allow it to go unnoticed. When he does, he wonders if it's an old note or a new note. His mind tells him one thing, his heart another, but his heart knows. Even though there are a million ways to explain the note. That it hardly passes as evidence. GM knows exactly how it came to be and what it means. He thinks "Not tomorrow, but someday I'll tell and give the note to Ilene."

Once outside, a full moon hangs in the sky, it's like a flashlight; it puts a faint light on everything. GM turns one last time towards the door he just secured and there Chenko stands.

M T remembers at this time Chenko is on low and moves his appearance power to medium, where it will stay. All the past attempts Chenko made combine in one final attempt with added power. He pops on like a light bulb. He's in full view, every bit of him. It's like he's standing in the light of a fire. Chenko for the first time can see in GM's eyes he's being seen. Both smile at each other, Chenko only able to repeat what is on the note. When GM reaches the tree line going home, he sees a kite hanging down from a tree, he'll come back and get it.

******

The crop circle incident put the barn on the map, there are few in the township who don't know where it is and for those coming in, it's not hard to find. The location is perfect; it offers plenty of parking and if the weather doesn't hold there's a place to go inside, if the weather does hold there's the opportunity for a bonfire. It's a good place to let your hair down in tribute to the deceased.

In the early morning of the wake the barn becomes a beehive of activity. Ilene and the girls are their along with a few very close friends, they set up the tables and food. Marbles drops by, leaves a ton of CD's and taps two kegs and puts them on ice. He's the first to pick up a new piece of hardware has been put on the vanity. He tells everyone he moved the vanity and that piece wasn't on it, setting the tone for the day. "He's here." It brings a smile to everyone.

There's a lull after everyone leaves and Chenko goes for a walk. He goes to the tree line and sees the kite GM saw. He decides to get it down and take it back to the barn. He likes it. Chenko gets to it before GM. He gets it down and when he gets back to the barn, he takes his time placing it, stands the white kite on the vanity; puts the file at its base to stabilize it. Chenko looks at it for a while and then goes out for another walk, maybe throw some rocks at the jay.

Chenko doesn't do this; instead, he walks to the field where the crop circle first appeared. Once there he looks back and sees he's in his office, but more than see, he feels himself in the office. It's the first time he realizes he's in two places at once. But it's not only field and office; he also feels he's in two dimensions at the same time.

He summons the office to the field and then puts himself at the entrance of the driveway while still in the field, experimenting. When he's done and one place at one time in the field, he begins to walk back to the barn, wondering if he can split his appearances. As he walks back the cars begin to pour in, one is a Mongo.

It's a real Whitman Sampler of people, for a hot late August afternoon, the hands on the clock move fast. The hands and the guests have no problem moving into the late evening and early morning and most stay. Ilene, Eve and Hope stay till about nine, they've heard all the stories and so far, they've been good, but feel if they stay any longer there's a possibility of hearing something they don't want to hear. Beer runs are starting, and the whiskey is running low, most staying are well oiled and it's just a question of time before the train leaves the tracks. Those with any sense would rather hear about it than see it.

Chenko follows them out and even though he's been told it won't happen, he keeps trying to appear to all of them. They're ready to put it to bed and move on. It's good, but brings Chenko to tears. They don't last long as he begins to understand this is the way it has to be. He watches them drive off, they weren't fine, but were okay. He'll come back to them in memories and dreams every chance he gets to make it better.

Eventually the loud music and the voices trying to talk above it break the spell. When he returns to the barn GM and Marbles are talking to Billy Kaloon and the guy, who dropped off the frozen pizza; who had the vanity plates, "Thorny?" GM is explaining the night of the kite and how it's a mystery how it's now on the vanity. Marbles explains the new hardware that finishes the piece, that wasn't on the piece he moved, the filings on the floor. The alcohol helps fuel the conversations to paranormal extremes. But Chenko is struck by the irony of what will later be perceived by their audience as fiction is basically true.

There are conversations by some late arrivals that hold his attention, he's tuned into every one of them, it's a strange feeling, but not a new one. Over in the corner Zoom is talking to Sneaky about the time they worked a strike. Chenko thinks "Zoom where you been?" touched he made the wake. He thinks of appearing, but he's looking for his brothers and sister. Chenko has to fight the urge. There are a ton of people he wants to appear in front of, big as life. The power is like a drug that can be used up fast, before you know it.

Every conversation he's hearing makes him want to appear to everyone. There are conversations where his stock has dropped a little as the night goes on, where he's being referred to as a son-of-a-bitch and bastard. He hears some of his friends from high school. One starts... "That son-of-a-bitch stole my girl sophomore year." It's overheard by a Barnnite, who doesn't even know him and drunk enough to tell him "Chenko could always talk to the split-tails." Like the guy shouldn't be surprised.

Another high school buddy remembers a flat he had one raw January night only to find out "The bastard stole the jack from my trunk."

There are more than a few of these conversations going on. Chenko can't deny any of them. If anything, Chenko is alright with them, for the most part they are followed by conversations of what he did to make up for them; it is good Ilene and the kids left when they did.

The conversations that really hold his interest go back to the third phase of his agenda, the Heroic Act. They're the ones about his terminal illness. He doesn't know who first brings it up, but it's a topic. There's a consensus from some that start out "You know Chenko...he was pushing that bike on that hill for a reason."

These are the people he most wants to appear before and tell them of the shock and awe. That he wasn't pushing anything, something just blew. That he was winning and would've made to eighty-eight, except for the sycamore. He wants to point out he got the sycamore that got him. The sycamore everyone carved their initials into, that took root the day he was born. The guy and tree they all know are both gone by a fate he didn't plan on. That he didn't make any decisions or take any actions on the Heroic Act.

Turns out those he appeared to at his wake weren't the ones he planned for, except for Linwood. He caught him in the office. He stood behind him and hit the power, appeared as big as life, maybe bigger. "You know what you took from here. You're in big trouble." Linwood collapses. It's enough to trigger a nine-one-one call when he's discovered, which in turn will lead to other discoveries about him. After the ambulance leaves, in the early morning the wake ends.

Aside from GM and Linwood, there's Ethel, Billy Kaloon's office assistant, Voegie, the garage door guy and Jimmy Chesterfield who see Chenko. Chenko himself can't even recall what they said to make him power an appearance. Before he knew it, he was out of them. The ones who see him are strange bedfellows that make what they tell others in the years to come more believable, than if these stories came from his brothers and sister. People might expect these stories from them, but not the others. Eventually all the strange and unexplainable events that occur during the calling hours, funeral and wake come back to his wife and kids over the years and become family lore.

M T sits in the Mongo waiting for Chenko. He sits there thinking maybe he overplayed his hand in choosing the Mongo, it's the only car left. "He doesn't have to search for it. Doesn't have to search for anything anymore," M T thinks to himself. Chenko sees it and for the first time realizes it's the car M T stopped with his thumb. This never occurred to him at the bridge and he has the feeling everything is coming full circle.

He gets in and tells M T how he messed up his appearances. Tells M T, in the end, he's not upset, more surprised. And he continues that even though they didn't go as planned, they weren't wasted. M T starts the Mongo. "Yeah, your last slice of life. Nothing turning out like you expected."

It makes Chenko aware of the time, space, atmosphere, constellations, fate, dimension and eternity that governed his life. Each of them is with its own flavor, each with its own characteristic, each working for or against him at different times.

The dog years of Ananias Zachenko are over. The wrist watch on the arm of time has been taken off. The ground and aerial views revealed. He didn't plan on any dog years, but once they came in view, he did plan and nothing turned out as expected. He's beginning to stir on the bed. Soon he'll be awake and his third and final dream will be over in this dimension, but just starting another dimension.

From here on out whatever a day is, a week, a month, a year will all change and time will only be known to God. From here on out each day, week, month, year will either be worse or better than the one before it, forever. For Chenko, he'll find it will be better. He's made weight. He kept some pieces on the board, now holds a card. They'll be a new agenda; he'll find the two hearts he has to give someone in eternity. It could've been clubs.

www.ingramcontent.com/pod-product-compliance
Lightning Source LLC
Chambersburg PA
CBHW060907120626
46553CB00001B/241